AQUA VITAE

T0151036

AQUA VITAE

A HISTORY OF THE SALOONS AND HOTEL BARS OF VICTORIA, 1851–1917

GLEN A. MOFFORD

TouchWood
Editions

TouchWood Editions
touchwoodeditions.com

LIBRARY AND ARCHIVES CANADA CATALOGUING IN PUBLICATION
Mofford, Glen, 1954–, author
Aqua vitae: a history of the saloons and hotel bars
of Victoria, 1851–1917/ Glen A. Mofford.

Includes index.
Issued in print and electronic formats.
ISBN 978-1-77151-189-6

1. Bars (Drinking establishments)—British Columbia—Victoria—
History. 2. Victoria (BC)—History—Anecdotes. I. Title.

TX950.59.C3M54 2016   647.95711'28   C2016-903367-8

Editing by Lana Okerlund
Proofreading by Cailey Cavallin
Design by Pete Kohut
Cover image #F-02562 courtesy of the Royal BC Museum and Archives (detail)
Author photo by Patti Doherty

We acknowledge the financial support of the Government of Canada through the Canada Book Fund (CBF) the Canada Council for the Arts, and the province of British Columbia through the Book Publishing Tax Credit.

The information in this book is true and complete to the best of the author's knowledge. All recommendations are made without guarantee on the part of the author. The author disclaims any liability in connection with the use of this information.

20 19 18 17 16   1 2 3 4 5

PRINTED IN CANADA AT FRIESENS

In memory of my parents, Jean and Larry Mofford,
and to my wife, Patti

CONTENTS

INTRODUCTION

Work is the curse of the drinking classes.[1]
—Oscar Wilde (1854–1900)

I n 1851 the first saloon opened in Victoria, and for the next
six-plus decades, saloons, along with hotel bars, formed
an intricate part of the social fabric of the city. Yet their
history has mostly been ignored by historians. Perhaps that
is because, like an iceberg of which one can see only the tip, most
of the history of Victoria's drinking establishments remains
hidden, an undiscovered mystery. Perhaps too many of the records
and stories about the saloons haven't survived over the years for
one reason or another. Perhaps the routine operations of the
saloons were thought to be too mundane for anyone to bother
keeping records. Whatever the reason for the historical gap, I
believe that the social history of Victoria's saloons and hotel bars
contains untold stories that, like gold nuggets found by some
lucky prospector, are treasures just waiting to be discovered.

That's not to say there hasn't been anything written about the history of Victoria's saloons and hotel bars; there has. A few significant events that took place in saloons or hotel bars over the years have been mentioned in passing in various articles or books, but those mentions were either too brief or limited in scope. There has not been a book written solely about the saloons and hotel bars of Victoria—until now.

From 1851 to 1917 hundreds of saloons and hotel bars dispensed alcohol twenty-four hours a day, seven days a week. While these establishments each featured a bar, spittoons, a bartender, and of course intoxicating liquors, they were otherwise quite different from one another. Forget about the one-dimensional saloons of the Wild West as depicted by Hollywood in countless movies and on television. The saloons of Victoria were much more complex and unique. Usually the tone of the bar was set by the personality of its proprietor, which could range from staid and sophisticated to downright raunchy and dangerous. The saloons in Victoria were a complex mix of various ethnic groups built upon American capital and entrepreneurship and British law and order.

Saloons were as numerous in nineteenth-century Victoria as coffee shops are today—one could be found on practically every corner. By 1909 there were over one hundred saloons and hotel bars in Victoria, each doing a roaring business. This book will give you a taste of what it was like to visit these saloons back in their heyday. You will be introduced to a cast of colourful characters who regularly inhabited the saloons and hotel bars. You will also discover what took place in the saloons, ranging from the humorous to the tragic, and all things in between.

The chapters in this book are organized chronologically, beginning with the pioneer saloons of the 1850s. Chapter One, "The Pioneer Saloons and Hotel Bars," traces the history of the first saloons that opened in Victoria, from James Yates's Ship Inn on Wharf Street to Bayley's Hotel, the first hotel in town. Due in part to being located on an island, Victoria was initially chosen as the site of the Hudson's Bay Company's headquarters in the Columbia District trading area. This gave the town a distinct advantage in defence and trade and as an important supplier for the flood of prospectors heading to the goldfields. The Fraser River Gold Rush that began in April 1858 gave the sleepy hamlet an economic boost as small businesses and a large concentration of saloons were built practically overnight. In addition to the prospectors making their way to the goldfields of the interior, you will rub shoulders with the sailors, sealers, whalers, and other seafarers who made up the majority of customers in the early saloons of Victoria.

Chapter Two, "The Rough Edge of Town," identifies the raunchiest saloons in the boom-and-bust times of the 1860s. Most of the notorious saloons were on Johnson Street, where no decent person would walk at night. But saloons could be found on nearly every corner of the downtown core. Here the occasional argument could quickly turn into a fight, and the outcome was sometimes fatal. There were also the more genteel saloons and hotel bars in which the proprietors did not put up with wild behaviour, where reading rooms and a restaurant were provided for their civilized patrons. The sheer number of saloons was staggering for the small population in Victoria at the time.

In Chapter Three, "Strictly First-Class," the histories of the most luxurious and high-class hotels and hotel bars are featured.

This chapter spans from the earliest lavish hotels of the 1860s to the magnificent Driard and Empress Hotels in the early twentieth century. Victoria was always a haven for tourists, especially from the mid-1880s on. Sophistication and technology greatly improved the hostelry industry, making for a number of truly fine and comfortable hotels.

Chapter Four, "The Golden Age," covers the period from 1870 to 1899, which I consider the golden age for saloons and hotel bars in Victoria. In this chapter a contrasting selection of saloons and hotel bars are profiled, each with its own unique qualities. This was the age when most everyone drank, and many drank to excess in an atmosphere of unrestricted delight. More saloons and hotel bars than ever before operated round-the-clock, with almost total impunity.

In Chapter Five, "Restriction to Prohibition," you will witness the rise of temperance movements in Victoria, which demanded that the evils wrought by the saloon be put in check or eliminated. This chapter covers the period from 1900 to 1917, when restrictions were placed on the hours that saloons were permitted to operate and liquor licences became more difficult to obtain. In 1911 saloon owners were warned that they would have to convert their businesses into hotels within three years. Most saloons closed as their proprietors simply couldn't afford such conversions. Those that did comply with the directive at great personal expense were dumbfounded when less than four years later their hotel bars were forced to close due to Prohibition, which came into effect on October 1, 1917. But some bars remained in business and attempted to sell products with low alcohol content.

This book is not a comprehensive, academic study of the saloon, but rather a series of true stories about the saloons and hotel bars of Victoria. I hope you will find the stories in this book interesting, informative, and exciting and that you will enjoy going back in time to the days of swinging doors, smoky bars, and five-cent beers.

THE PIONEER SALOONS AND HOTEL BARS

1851–59

In wine there is wisdom, in beer there is freedom,
in water there is bacteria.[1]

—Benjamin Franklin (1706–1790)

1. Ship Inn Saloon (first location)
2. Ship Inn Saloon (second location)
3. Bayley's Hotel
4. Phoenix Hotel and Saloon
5. Victoria Hotel
6. Boomerang Inn
7. Royal Hotel
8. California Saloon
9. What Cheer House
10. Metropolitan to Colonial Hotel

In 1850 Victoria was a tiny colony on the southern tip of Vancouver Island administered by the Hudson's Bay Company. The company's fort dominated the landscape, and scattered outside its walls were a few residential and commercial buildings. Great Britain urged the Hudson's Bay Company to promote immigration, and gradually a small village began to develop.

Drinking alcohol was a part of life in Victoria, as it was all over North America in the nineteenth century. Consuming spirits and beer was not only accepted in society but also popular, and the products were readily available and relatively inexpensive. "Adults drank at home, at work and at play, usually every day and often all day."[2] Most people believed that drinking a moderate amount of alcohol daily was good for their health. Alcohol was both nutritious and helpful as a natural painkiller. Spirits were considered aqua vitae, the "water of life," whereas actual water had quite the opposite reputation. Europeans remembered the devastating, water-borne cholera epidemics that had swept through their homelands and taken a heavy toll in lives. Water was usually dirty and was risky to drink (due to bacteria) unless it was boiled and served as tea or coffee.

James Yates was one of the pioneer businessmen who built his home and business outside the walls of the fort. Originally drawn from Scotland to Victoria to work as a ship carpenter with the Hudson's Bay Company, Yates broke out of his contract, for which he served a jail sentence of thirty days, to gain the freedom to pursue his own business goals. He purchased two lots, just northwest of the fort at what eventually were named Yates and Wharf Streets, where he built his home and the first saloon in Victoria—the Ship Inn.

Business was brisk at the Ship Inn Saloon, and two more saloons soon opened in the tiny but growing community. James Douglas, in his dual role as governor of Vancouver Island and chief factor for the Hudson's Bay Company, sorely needed to find new sources of revenue to pay for improvements and infrastructure. In March 1853 Douglas introduced a bill to tax the wholesale and retail sale of liquor. This meant that saloon owners had to pay an annual fee of £120 for their retail liquor licence. As soon as the new licensing fee became law in July that same year, the competing saloons closed their doors, leaving the Ship Inn Saloon to enjoy a brief monopoly.

The first census compiled by Douglas in December 1854 recorded 232 residents, 79 houses, and 12 businesses in Victoria. Town lots and a street grid were surveyed by J.D. Pemberton. Regular town lots were 60 feet by 120 feet and sold for fifty dollars each. Most of the early buildings were rough, hand-hewn log structures. A few exceptions were buildings that were made from material shipped, at great expense, from the mills in San Francisco. The What Cheer House that opened on the southwest corner of Yates and Blanshard Streets was built with lumber milled in California. Victoria was growing, but ever so slowly.

The Pacific Squadron of the Royal Navy moved its base

from Chile to the deep-water inlet of Esquimalt in 1854 while Great Britain and Russia were entangled in the Crimean War. The Royal Navy base at Esquimalt gave businesses in Victoria a much-needed boost. This was the beginning of an important relationship between the Royal Navy and the development of Esquimalt and Victoria. The Royal Navy brought approximately $500,000 worth of business into the Victoria economy each year, while her sailors kept many saloons and hotel bars afloat.[3] The local saloons were soon filled with thirsty, raucous sailors who became regular patrons at their favourite watering holes.

Until 1857 there were no formal hotels in Victoria. Charles Bayley opened the first on the corner of Yates and Government Streets. The two-storey wooden structure was a modest establishment with nine beds on the upper floor. It catered mostly to working-class men such as seafarers, miners, and the occasional farmer who needed to rest up after an evening in the saloon. The saloon and restaurant were on street level.

Victoria was a quiet village with only a handful of shops, a few saloons, and the Bayley's Hotel until an event occurred in the spring of 1858 that permanently changed everything. On Sunday morning, April 25, 1858, the ship *Commodore* arrived in Victoria Harbour from San Francisco carrying the first load of miners who would flood into Victoria to obtain mining licences and supplies for their journey to the Fraser River Gold Rush. "The gold rush was the catalyst which made British Columbia a province and provided the wealth and population that made Victoria a city."[4]

The population of Victoria doubled on that day, and more gold seekers were on their way. Over the next seven months, twenty thousand people arrived in Victoria on their way to the goldfields.

The city fathers were overwhelmed by this flood of humanity (mostly Americans dreaming of making it rich), and were hard pressed to find accommodations for all of the new arrivals. The one hotel in town filled up quickly. A tent city grew overnight, and food and other goods became scarce and expensive. The existing saloons were not enough to quench the thirst of so many new customers, so new saloons opened. One clever businessman, the newly arrived American Thomas McCann, purchased a temporary liquor licence and sold liquor out of his tent while his Phoenix Saloon was under construction on Yates Street. A shot of liquor sold for twelve and a half cents and a mug of beer went for five cents.

The effect that the Fraser River Gold Rush had on Victoria cannot be overstated. Once Victorians recovered from the great influx of prospectors, they got caught up in land speculation, where prices virtually changed hourly.[5] In a space of six weeks, 225 buildings were erected. Goods and services began arriving from San Francisco, which helped relieve any shortages. The bulk of the new saloons opened on Yates, Government, and Bastion Streets, with exciting names such as the California, the Phoenix, the Miner's Exchange, the Union, the Fashion, and the Capital. New hotels opened as well, including the Victoria Hotel, the first brick building in town. The Royal, American, and Colonial Hotels all opened between the summer of 1858 and the spring of 1859.

Along with the new saloons and hotel bars came the drunkards and hooligans, a part of every boom town. Most miners left Victoria as soon as they purchased their mining licences and supplies, but others lingered on for weeks, drinking in the saloons and roaming the streets at all hours of the day and night. One in three arrests was for drunk and disorderly conduct. While these statistics were alarming, it was easy for the police to spot and apprehend a drunk.

Many saloons came and went, and some fly-by-night proprietors didn't even bother purchasing liquor licences. But a handful of saloons and hotel bars from the 1850s stood out from the rest. These establishments set down roots in the community and enjoyed a loyal customer base for years. The following is a look at the more significant pioneer saloons and hotel bars, beginning with the first saloon to open in Victoria: the Ship Inn.

SHIP INN SALOON
1851–62

James Stuart Yates was born in Linlithgow, Scotland, on January 21, 1819. He signed on with the Hudson's Bay Company as a ship carpenter in 1848; that same year, Yates married Mary Powell of Montgomeryshire. Two weeks later they began their journey to Fort Victoria on the ship *Harpooner*.[6]

Yates grew to dislike the strict discipline and heavy-handedness of the Hudson's Bay Company, and after eighteen months he escaped to the goldfields of California. Upon his return Yates was charged with breach of contract and sentenced to six months in the northeast bastion of Fort Victoria, which was used as a makeshift jail. Yates served thirty days of his sentence, and upon

Looking south on Wharf Street from Yates Street, 1860. James Yates's second Ship Inn Saloon is the stone building on the right in the photograph.
IMAGE #A-00726 COURTESY OF THE ROYAL BC MUSEUM AND ARCHIVES

his release was discharged from the Hudson's Bay Company. He was granted independent status on January 29, 1851. This suited the stubborn Yates, and he wasted little time in pursuing his business goals.

On June 9, 1851, Yates paid fifty pounds for each of two undeveloped waterfront lots, 201 and 202, on Wharf Street, northwest of the fort. There he built his home and the first privately owned saloon in Victoria, the Ship Inn.[7] Unfortunately, there are no known surviving photographs or illustrations of his saloon, but the location was most likely 1252 Wharf Street at the southwest corner with what eventually was named Yates Street.[8]

The Ship Inn Saloon did a tremendous business, with the only competition coming from the Hudson's Bay Company store. For a few months Yates enjoyed a monopoly on the retail liquor business before two other saloons opened. His main customers were seafarers, such as sealers, sailors, and fishers, who came in to enjoy a five-cent mug of beer or a twelve-and-a-half-cent shot of liquor.

From 1851 until the summer of 1853, the saloon business was unregulated and a licence was not required to sell spirits or beer. Two more saloons opened before Sir James Douglas, the chief factor of the colony, introduced a revenue bill that called for a licensing system for the wholesale and retail sale of alcohol. The annual fee for a retail licence was set at £120, while wholesale licences cost £100. The bill passed into law in July 1853 and resulted in the closure of the two saloons competing with the Ship Inn. Yates enjoyed a monopoly once more.

Profits from his liquor business allowed Yates to buy up town lots on Langley, Wharf, and Yates Streets, the last ultimately bearing his name. By 1860 James Yates was one of the wealthiest men in Victoria. That same year, Yates closed his saloon and reopened it a few doors to the south, at 1218 Wharf Street, a newly completed stone and brick building that still exists. The lower level was a warehouse for merchandise, primarily cases of liquor that were brought in directly off ships moored in Victoria Harbour. The bar in the Ship Inn was on street level. The new Ship Inn would last about a year before Yates closed it and returned to his native Scotland to see to his son's education. The saloon was converted into an auction house by the new owners.

At least four Ship Inn Saloons operated in Greater Victoria between 1851 and 1869. James Yates owned the first two, followed by a Ship Inn Saloon in Esquimalt and another Ship Inn on Wharf Street just across from where Yates's second saloon had been located. They all did extremely well, attracting a loyal customer base that allowed these establishments to prosper for years. In Chapter Four, "The Golden Age," we will take a look at the fourth Ship Inn Saloon.

BAYLEY'S HOTEL
1857–73

Charles Alfred Bayley opened the first hotel in Victoria in 1857 on the northeast corner of Yates and Government Streets. The modest two-storey Bayley's Hotel was a wooden structure that offered nine beds on the upper floor and catered to working-class men such as seafarers, miners, and tradesmen.

BAYLEY HOTEL,

Corner Yates and Government Streets,

VICTORIA, V. I.

CHAS. A. BAYLEY, - - - PROPRIETOR.

BOARD and LODGING on the most reasonable terms.

Charles Alfred Bayley and Bayley's Hotel, the first hotel in Victoria.
DAILY COLONIST (DATE UNKNOWN)

A saloon and restaurant were on the main floor. A sign hung above the hotel entrance advertising the specialty of the house: fresh oysters available for lunch or dinner. This was primarily meant for out-of-town guests, as most locals knew that oysters were plentiful in Victoria and one could easily gather them for free.

Bayley arrived in Victoria aboard the *Tory* in 1850 from Essex, England. Though he signed a five-year contract as a labourer for the Hudson's Bay Company, James Douglas found Bayley more suitable as a teacher, and appointed him schoolmaster for the Nanaimo District in 1852.[9] Bayley became the first schoolteacher in Nanaimo. He married two years later, then moved to Victoria in 1856, having completed his five-year term with the company.

Bayley opened a grocery store in Victoria, but was soon

convinced by a friend to try his hand at running a hotel. The Bayley's Hotel opened in 1857, and his timing could not have been better. Only a few months later, thousands of men came to Victoria to take part in the Fraser River Gold Rush. More than 450 men disembarked from the first ship of gold seekers, and Bayley's Hotel quickly filled to beyond capacity and remained busy all year long.

The *Colonist* newspaper best describes the scene inside Bayley's Hotel: "When the rush came in 1858 the upper flat, a mere loft, was furnished with cots and straw mattresses, and there the early gold seekers were wont to stretch their weary limbs at two dollars per head and gasp for breath in a fetid and overcharged atmosphere till the morning light forced its way into the apartment through the tiny windows on the Yates Street side." [10]

That summer Bayley leased the saloon portion of the business to John C. Keenan, who dispensed cocktails at two bits (twenty-five cents) per glass at the bar. Water was extremely rare during the dry summer months, the supply coming from Spring Ridge in Fairfield, some four miles away. Water in wooden barrels was delivered around town by horse carts. Consequently, there was a bit-per-glass charge for water at most bars in town. The price for a glass of water at the Bayley's Hotel was fifteen cents. When one customer complained, remarking that water should be free, the barkeeper retorted, "See here young feller, be lucky you don't pay fifty cents for a drink of water, it's cheap at fifteen cents." [11]

Victoria was a boom town. While most of the gold seekers stayed only long enough to purchase their mining licences and supplies, others lingered in the many new saloons and hotel bars.

Along with the economic boom came a dramatic increase in crime. Most arrests were for public intoxication, fighting, and theft. The Bayley's Hotel was not immune, and in the early morning hours of Saturday, December 17, 1859, a robbery took place at the hotel. The perpetrator[s] entered through an unlocked window and stole clothes, blankets, and money from the guests while they were sleeping. No one was arrested for the crime.[12]

Bayley sold his hotel in 1860 and devoted his time to politics. By 1865 he suffered from ill health and decided to move his family to Dallas, Oregon. Meanwhile, the Bayley's Hotel closed and became a meat market until 1874, when new owners changed it back to a bar called the San Francisco Saloon, leased to William H. Thistle. For many years the corner of Yates and Government was known as "the Thistle Corner." In 1883 the old Bayley's Hotel building was purchased by Thomas Trounce and demolished to make way for the Pritchard House, a palatial three-storey brick hotel.

PHOENIX HOTEL AND SALOON
1858–81

A great number of new saloons opened during the gold rush years of 1858 to 1862, but none were as unique as the Phoenix Hotel and Saloon.

The Phoenix first opened in a tent set up along muddy Yates Street during the early stage of the Fraser River Gold Rush.

PHŒNIX SALOON,

ESTABLISHED IN 1858.

THE UNDERSIGNED informs his numerous patrons and the public generally that he has received by recent arrivals direct from England, a selection of CHOICE

BRANDIES, GIN,

JAMAICA RUM,

Irish & Scotch Whiskey, Alsopp's Ale on draught,

BYAS AND HIBBERT'S PORTER, IN BOTTLES;

Also, a Choice Article of BOURBON WHISKEY direct from San Francisco, Cal.

IRISH AND SCOTCH HOT WHISKEY PUNCHES AND TOM AND JERRYS MADE TO ORDER.
Every honest working man who may favor me with his patronage, may depend upon getting a glass of good Liquor in my Saloon.
FRESH OYSTERS direct from Sooke always on hand.

T. H. McCANN, Proprietor.

Advertisement from the 1863 *British Columbia and Victoria Guide and Directory*, compiled and published by Frederick P. Howard and George Barnett.

Thomas H. McCann was one of the thousands of Americans to arrive in Victoria hoping to cash in on the gold rush. He managed to purchase a liquor licence and sold liquor out of a large tent while his saloon was being built on the northeast corner of Waddington and Yates Streets.

The non-tent version of the Phoenix Saloon opened in July 1858. McCann's saloon was a single-storey wooden building, where he sold liquor, cigars, a "hot lunch every day," and mugs of beer. The Phoenix had a long mahogany bar to belly up to, or patrons could choose to "sit down and be happy." Fresh oysters from Sooke were always on hand, and to remain competitive, McCann began to offer free lunches daily to any customer who purchased a drink. Shortly after the saloon opened, McCann added a reading room for patrons who wanted a quiet place to enjoy a drink and a Havana cigar while leafing through a favourite book or catching up on world news from London, New York, or San Francisco.

There were very few regulations in the saloons, and age

restrictions were non-existent in the heady days of the gold rush, as evidenced by the following advertisement from 1859: "Wanted: a young lad twelve to sixteen years old to wash glasses and to make himself generally useful. Apply at the Phoenix Saloon."[13]

McCann expanded his business in 1861 with the addition of a hotel and a spacious restaurant. The dinner menu improved as the Phoenix Hotel and Saloon became more sophisticated. Customers could choose from a variety of soups that would complement their meal, such as mock turtle, clam chowder, ox tail, or vegetable. The choices of liquor improved as well, with the addition of fine French brandies; English, Spanish, and California wines; English ale and porter draught on tap or in bottles; and a large selection of liquors. During the Christmas season of 1862, the Phoenix Hotel and Saloon offered up fat turkeys and chickens served with gallons of eggnog.

McCann sold the Phoenix to William P. Marsh in 1864. The business then changed hands many times until 1881. The last owner of the Phoenix Hotel and Saloon was Mrs. Walter Broughner. An advertisement in the local paper read, "The Phoenix saloon, Yates and Waddington streets, has passed into the hands of Mrs. Broughner. Enough said, the mere mention of the fact conveys a guarantee of good accommodation and fair dealing."[14] Clearly the saloon and hotel business was not solely man's domain. There were a number of very successful women acting as either owners or proprietors in Victoria at the time, and many of these amazing women will be discussed in upcoming chapters.

The Phoenix Hotel and Saloon closed in 1881 and was demolished to make way for a large brick produce warehouse.

VICTORIA HOTEL
1858–78

The Victoria Hotel was opened by George Richardson in August 1858 on the northeast corner of Courtney and Government Streets. It was the first brick building in what would become British Columbia. Twenty-three-year-old Richardson arrived in Victoria aboard the *Norman Morison* from Gravesend, England, in 1850.[15] He worked for the Hudson's Bay Company, where he earned enough money to purchase three hundred acres of land.

In 1858 Richardson returned to England, where he married Mary Ann Parker. Richardson brought his wife to Victoria, arriving just before the gold rush in April 1858. Richardson had planned to work on his farm, located just outside of town, but he changed his plans when he saw what a lucrative opportunity opening a hotel could be. The Victoria Hotel was a modest two-storey brick building with six rooms on the upper floor and a saloon and adjoining parlour on the ground floor.

Hotels and saloons not only were places for drinking and sleeping, but also served the young community in many other ways. The Victoria Hotel provided a place for organizations to hold their meetings; the Independent Order of Odd Fellows (IOOF), for example, used the Victoria Hotel until leasing their own building a few years later. The Shipwrights & Caulkers Union and the Pioneer Cricket Club also met at the Victoria Hotel. Richardson organized elaborate dinners to celebrate special occasions such as Queen Victoria's birthday and a

The Windsor Hotel, in 1885, opened in 1858 as the
Victoria Hotel, the first brick building in Victoria.

"Race Dinner" that preceded the annual horse race at Beacon Hill Park. Richardson also held raffles in which practically every farm animal imaginable was raffled off, from fat turkeys and geese at Christmas to race horses, rabbits, pigs, and an interesting mix of other animals. For fifty cents, one lucky ticket holder could win an excellent three-course dinner. Raffles and giveaways would soon be commonplace in many saloons in the city, but Richardson started the practice at the Victoria Hotel.

The Victoria Hotel also served as a makeshift hospital. In 1864 a man accidentally shot himself with his own shotgun near the hotel and was taken into one of the hotel rooms to be treated for his wounds.[16] In another incident a man was stabbed out in the street and staggered into the Victoria Hotel, bloodied and in dire need of medical attention. On another occasion two combatants were found exhausted and bloodied in the back of the hotel after a confrontation. An eyewitness said that the men "mauled each other's faces and tore the clothes off their backs." When they were separated, they "adjourned to take a drink."[17]

In 1864 Richardson leased the Victoria Hotel to John Gowan; a few months later Dan McBride took over the lease. McBride operated the Victoria Hotel until 1866 when Richardson returned.

Perhaps the single most exciting event that took place at the hotel, certainly an event that has been well written about through the years, was when Richardson accidentally blew up the place. One Friday evening in the autumn of 1876 as Richardson was preparing for bed, he was alerted to a foul smell coming from the downstairs parlour. He went to investigate, carrying with him a lit candle to find his way. Unfortunately, he walked into a room filled with gas, which immediately ignited and caused a terrible explosion. The blast resulted in Richardson receiving severe burns to his face, head, and one hand. The explosion shattered windows, burned the window blinds and curtains, and singed the wallpaper. It also caused a lamppost on the corner of Fort and Government Streets to topple over. Alarmed hotel guests jumped out of bed and frantically climbed down to the street from the second-storey balcony. One guest, while attending to his family, lost his balance and fell onto the road below, fracturing his elbow. It was later discovered that recent renovations to the parlour had ruptured one of the gas pipes and caused a slow, quiet gas leak.[18]

In 1878 the Victoria Hotel was leased to Benjamin Pitt Griffin, who had just sold his Boomerang Inn, located near Bastion and Langley Streets. Griffin changed the name to the Boomerang Hotel and conducted business under that name until 1885, when the name of the hotel changed again to the Windsor Hotel. Richardson continued to be the owner, but he preferred to lease his hotel out until he finally sold it in 1903 and retired to his home in James Bay.

BOOMERANG INN
1858–78

Benjamin and Adelaide Griffin travelled from England to Victoria, taking the long way via Australia and San Francisco and arriving in 1858. Benjamin Pitt Griffin had gone to California to try his

Benjamin Pitt Griffin, proprietor of the Boomerang Inn.
IMAGE #G-05177 COURTESY OF THE ROYAL BC MUSEUM AND ARCHIVES

luck in the goldfields but had ended up opening the Boomerang Saloon in San Francisco. He earned a reputation as a fair and honest man. His business did well until 1858, when he was lured by the call of gold once more during the Fraser River Gold Rush. He sold his business in California and moved to Victoria, where he opened the Boomerang Inn at Court Alley and Bastion Street, in an area now known as Bastion Square.

The Griffins were genial hosts. Adelaide put together free bologna sandwiches for the patrons of the Boomerang bar, while Ben served up mugs of strong ale. The Boomerang was a two-storey wooden structure with a large false front and a few rooms upstairs.

On the main floor were the bar, a small reading room, a restaurant, and a meeting room.

The inn was located near the jailhouse and courthouse, so many of the customers were lawyers, policemen, courthouse employees, and the accused. Hangings took place at the back of the jail, and a few of these unfortunate convicted individuals were permitted a last good, stiff drink at the Boomerang Inn bar before being sent to their maker. "Public executions were one of Victoria's more lugubrious forms of entertainment until they were abolished in 1870."[19]

Aside from his duties as a hotelier, Griffin was also one of the original members of the Victoria Amateur Club, an acting group, and occasionally performed at the nearby Royal Theatre. Griffin provided a room in his inn for club meetings.[20] He was also a prolific reader, and he took great pride in the collection of books and periodicals found in his reading room, which was attached to the inn. He often read out loud to an appreciative audience, and years later he started book raffles.

In July 1861 Adelaide Griffin died at the youthful age of thirty-one. Ben Griffin was now a widower, left to raise their daughter, Grace. When Grace was of school age she was sent to San Francisco for her education. She eventually met a man, and they married on February 15, 1872.[21]

A large part of the success of the Boomerang Inn was due to Ben Griffin's personality. He was outgoing, honest, and genuine. He was obviously in the right business, as he was well liked by his customers and enjoyed a good reputation in the community. Griffin liked to advertise his business in a most unusual and clever way, as revealed by such advertisements in the local newspaper:

"Not true that Ben Griffin was shot in the fight with the Samalchas of Cowichan. He still lives at the Boomerang."[22] While tending bar, Griffin would burst into song when the mood struck him or leave his customers in fits of laughter from one of his many stories. Griffin followed politics and the news of the day, and he always had an opinion to share with whoever would listen.

In February 1878 Griffin sold the Boomerang Inn and leased George Richardson's Victoria Hotel on the corner of Government and Courtney Streets. He was given permission to rename the hotel the Boomerang Hotel. Many of his regular customers followed him there, and Griffin continued to be very successful while he dispensed humour and political views with pints of beer.

On Sunday morning, August 7, 1881, Ben Griffin died at the age of seventy-two following a four-month illness. By his bedside were his daughter and the rest of the family, along with his many friends and admirers. There was a tremendous turnout for the funeral of this well-loved and respected pioneer. Ben Griffin was buried at the Ross Bay Cemetery. A tombstone in memory of his wife, Adelaide, the inscription of which is barely visible today, can be found at Pioneer Park in Victoria.

ROYAL HOTEL
1858–74

The Royal Hotel was the second brick building to open in Victoria, losing out to the Victoria Hotel by only a few months. It opened on October 13, 1858, with an elaborate celebration held

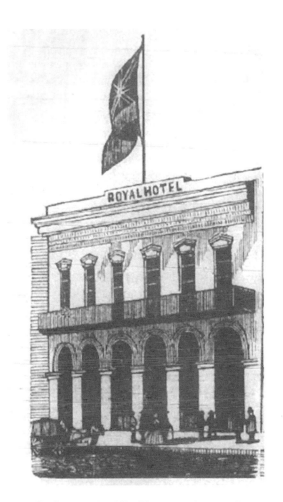

The Royal Hotel on Wharf Street was the second
brick building completed in Victoria, 1858.
ILLUSTRATION FROM THE *VICTORIA DIRECTORY*, 1860

in the newly completed, spacious ballroom. James Wilcox was the first proprietor of the Royal Hotel, a two-storey brick building on the east side of Wharf Street near the corner with Johnson Street. Wilcox was a successful businessman who owned four properties on Kane and Fort Streets. He also had $10,000 worth of shares in a Cariboo gold mine.[23] The hotel offered luxurious rooms with a view for overnight guests or board and lodging for ten dollars per week. There was fine dining in the restaurant managed by Mrs. Dunlevey, as well as private rooms for families, a large hall for balls or meetings, and of course a fully stocked bar complete with billiard tables.

Wilcox advertised extensively, and the ballroom was fully booked for months in advance. Wilcox also gave back to the community by hosting a ball in aid of the Royal Hospital Fund; the three dollars per ticket, which included a splendid supper, went directly to the charity.[24]

Everything appeared to be going well for Wilcox and his Royal Hotel until the autumn of 1865, when he began experiencing financial difficulties. Things went badly so quickly that Wilcox had little choice but to file for bankruptcy on November 30, 1865. To make matters worse, the following month, while doing repairs to his roof, Wilcox fell from his ladder and broke a rib.[25] Sophia Hill, his sister-in-law, operated the hotel for the next two years while Wilcox was on the mend and dealing with his creditors.

James Wilcox made his comeback in 1868 and successfully ran the Royal Hotel until 1873, when he took some time away from his business to work a gold mine in Dease Lake. He died there in July 1874. Mrs. Wilcox took over the business until it was sold that autumn.

The old Royal Hotel reopened as an import and export business. In November 1877 William Jensen purchased the business and reopened the old hostelry as the Occidental Hotel, which soon expanded northward along Wharf Street to the corner of Johnson Street, swallowing up the old wood buildings along the way. The Royal Hotel building had a new lease on life as the popular Occidental Hotel (see Chapter Four), which would last for many years.

CALIFORNIA SALOON
1858–1917

The California Saloon opened on the southwest corner of Johnson and Waddington Streets during the heady days of the gold rush in 1858. The California was one of the many American-owned businesses that opened during that period, and one of the most successful. Initially it opened as a small wooden structure owned by partners named LeLaire and Bickle, but it was eventually demolished and replaced with a handsome brick building in 1888.

The California Saloon was not fancy, but it did provide customers with an excellent selection of liquors and cigars and an extra room complete with a billiard table. An advertisement in the local newspaper read, "A pool game will be played and first prize will be a splendid French revolver and a surprise for the remainder of the players." [26] I never did find out what they meant by a "surprise for the remainder of the players." Billiards was a very popular pastime and was available in

The California Saloon, 529 Johnson Street.

most saloons and hotels at the time. A substantial amount of money changed hands in both casual and organized billiards competition. There were prizes for the winners, and a few good players made names for themselves, gaining respect from their peers along with bragging rights. Billiards was so popular that the government began selling licences to saloon owners at ten dollars annually for the first billiard table and five dollars for each additional table.

Johnson Street was the northern edge of town back in the 1860s and had more saloons and hotel bars than any other area of town. A rough place at times, the California Saloon fit into the rowdy drinking, gambling, and fighting saloons found on Johnson Street. On one occasion, while the bartender and some regular customers were outside the saloon watching a dogfight, a lone customer in the bar decided to raid the safe but was caught in the process. On another occasion two thieves managed to rob the till, but they were chased along Cormorant Street and caught by the bartender. In March 1861 a sailor was fined for breaking in the door of the saloon while on a drunken rampage. These are just a few examples of the fun that took place at the lively California Saloon.

Each saloon and hotel bar reflected the personality of its owner or bartender. Andy Bechtel, who enjoyed wearing a tasselled smoking cap, was the California Saloon's well-known no-nonsense bartender and proprietor in the late 1890s. He delighted in tossing recalcitrant sailors into the street.[27] Consistently one of the rowdiest in town, the saloon developed a bad reputation with incidents like the following, which was reported in the newspaper: "A Lively Racket—At eight o'clock last evening a couple of 'sluggers' got at each other at the California Saloon and several rounds were fought, several others who seemed spoiling for a fight took hand, and it looked at one time as if there was going to be a free fight." [28]

An interesting note about the California Saloon is that there was a piano in the corner of the room at which different players would be paid to entertain patrons between fist-fights. One of those piano players, named little Annie Rooney, was a transgender man who once served in the United States Navy for six months before his birth sex, as female, was discovered. [29]

The owners of the infamous California Saloon added a hotel that lasted until October 1917, when Prohibition shut it down. The building later became part of the Salvation Army complex and was eventually demolished.

WHAT CHEER HOUSE
1858–66

Thomas and Sarah Williams ran a gristmill in Yreka, California, but headed to Victoria in 1858, attracted by the gold rush. Immediately seeing the need for a hotel, they ordered lumber milled in and shipped from San Francisco for their enterprise. The What Cheer House opened on the southwest corner of Yates and Blanshard Streets in what was until recently the parking lot for the Dalton Hotel. The name "What Cheer" was taken from the famously successful hotel in San Francisco at the time. [30]

Advertisement for the What Cheer House, *British Colonist*.

The couple had ten children before disaster struck.[31] Shortly after the hotel was completed, Thomas suffered a paralytic stroke and remained disabled until his death in 1871. Sarah ran the business and looked after their large family, an extraordinary feat by an exceptional pioneer woman. The Williamses sold the hotel to Thomas Mitchell in 1862 and moved to the Cowichan area, allowing Sarah to tend to her ailing husband.

Thomas Mitchell and his wife, Margaret (née Jenkins), both came from Swansea, Wales, where they married in 1851. In 1862 they decided to immigrate to Victoria aboard the *Sylatria*. The long voyage took four months and eighteen days.[32] After purchasing the What Cheer House, the Mitchells operated it together for only a brief time before Thomas was lured by the Cariboo Gold Rush, leaving Margaret to operate the hotel on her own. Upon his return the Mitchells had saved enough money to open a dry-goods store on Johnson Street. The hotel again went up for sale and was purchased by John Smith.

In 1866 the What Cheer House went up for auction. Fortunately, there is an excellent description of the hotel at that time. The hostelry was located at (104) Yates Street on a regular town lot, number 106, which was 60 feet by 120 feet.[33]

The three-storey building offered a large dining room that could accommodate up to one hundred guests, a full kitchen, a large hall, and a pantry in the basement. Two sitting rooms and five bedrooms were on the main floor, and the upper floor consisted of nine guest rooms. There was also a three-room guest cottage on the property as well as a three-room bathhouse containing four bathing tubs and one steam bath with a large tank in the rear. "The premises and bathing room are supplied with a never failing well of pure water" plus "the usual outhouses for a well organized establishment."[34]

There appears to be no record of what happened to the What Cheer House after 1866. In 1876 Mrs. Gerow was operating the Dominion House on a portion of the site where the What Cheer House once stood, but the place may have been in business under the Dominion House name as early as 1870. The Dominion House, later renamed the Dominion Hotel, developed into one of the most successful hotels in Victoria and is described in detail in Chapter Three. The pioneer businesswoman Sarah Williams, the original owner of the What Cheer House, died on June 24, 1907, in Victoria at the age of ninety-two. She outlived all of her ten children.

METROPOLITAN TO COLONIAL HOTEL
1859–73

The last of the significant hotels of the 1850s is the Metropolitan Hotel, which C. York opened on Government Street between

Yates and View Streets in January 1859. The January advertisement in the newspaper promised carpeted rooms with comfortable feather beds and stoves throughout. Board started at eight dollars per week; the rate for room and board was set from ten to thirteen dollars per week.[35] This hotel should not be confused with the Colonial-Metropole Hotel that existed at 551 Johnson Street from 1883 to 1911.

The Metropolitan Hotel lasted only six months before the new owners, Henry Kraft and Thomas F. Tighe, changed the name to the Colonial Hotel and Restaurant in June 1859. Kraft and Tighe purchased two billiard tables for the large saloon they added to the main floor of the hotel, and advertised every week in the local newspaper. The Colonial Hotel and Restaurant was actually two buildings connected by a hall. The hotel and saloon were in one building, while the restaurant was in the other. The building that served as hotel and saloon started out as a hotel in Whatcom County, Washington Territory, back in 1857. Henry Kraft had the hotel dismantled and rebuilt in Victoria beside the new Metropolitan Hotel.[36]

The saloon was leased to Prosper Grelley and the restaurant was leased to Sosthenes Driard, a chef and entrepreneur hailing from France. Driard quickly gained a reputation for being among the best chefs in town, with his "corpulence . . . a tribute to the quality of his cuisine."[37]

With the Colonial Hotel doing well and the saloon and restaurant making a tidy profit, Henry Kraft bought out his partner to become the sole owner of the business in 1860. In February 1861 a disagreement between Kraft and Grelley, who leased the saloon, was resolved in the courts in favour of Kraft,

The Colonial and Metropolitan Hotels, Government Street.

but it cost Kraft so much money that he had to recover his costs by selling the hotel at auction in August 1861. The new owner was chef Sosthenes Driard.

Driard had gained respect for his excellent restaurant, and now the public was in for an additional treat. Driard hired a French barber and opened a hairdressing salon attached to the hotel. He also added the Gipsey House, where one could purchase the finest ice cream and strawberries, chocolates, cakes, and coffee to go along with his magnificent dinners.[38] The public reaction was marvellous, and Driard made a small fortune from these additional businesses.

One evening a stovepipe in the hotel collapsed, causing a small fire. Although the damage was minimal, Driard decided that to protect his investment, he would demolish both the hotel and restaurant and rebuild with brick. In the summer of 1864 Driard hired a contractor to begin improvements to his business. The restaurant was to be replaced first, followed by the hotel, then the saloon, and finally the adjoining businesses.[39]

The grand opening of the new Colonial Hotel took place in July 1866. An elaborately decorated first-class restaurant opened on the main floor, and a large room, named the Vancouver Club, opened on the second floor, complete with a bar and new billiard tables. The Vancouver Club operated out of the second floor of the Colonial Hotel from 1866 to 1871. After 1871 it became the Colonial Hotel billiards room.[40]

In 1871 Driard purchased the St. George Hotel located on View Street between Broad and Douglas Streets. He changed the name of the hotel to the Colonial Hotel Branch, but most people called it Driard's House. Much more will be revealed about the Driard Hotel and Sosthenes Driard in Chapter Three.

In 1873 the old Vancouver Club above the restaurant in the Colonial Hotel, now a billiards room, became known as the Jockey Club Saloon. The saloon kept the three billiard tables for patrons to enjoy, and business went well until a catastrophic event occurred. Just after two in the morning on Monday, June 7, 1875, a fire broke out in the Jockey Club Saloon. According to eye witnesses, flames consumed the hotel so quickly that only a few items inside the hotel could be salvaged before staff and customers had to run for their lives. The police and firefighters concentrated their efforts on saving the adjoining businesses as the Colonial Hotel fire was too intense and advanced to save the structure.[41]

There was no loss of life, but the Colonial Hotel was destroyed. Driard did not live to witness the terrifying end of his beloved hotel, as he passed away in February 1873 (see Chapter Three).

The early 1850s saw the first saloon in Victoria, but it was the Fraser River Gold Rush that gave rise to a variety of changes in the sleepy company town and triggered the number of saloons and hotel bars doing booming business by the end of the decade.

The story of Victoria's saloons and hotel bars took an ominous turn in the 1860s. We move now to the most notorious and despicable saloons and hotel bars in "The Rough Edge of Town," and to the mysterious secret found under the floorboards of the Omineca Saloon.

CHAPTER TWO

THE ROUGH EDGE OF TOWN

1860–69

Sometimes too much to drink is barely enough.
—Mark Twain (1835–1910)[1]

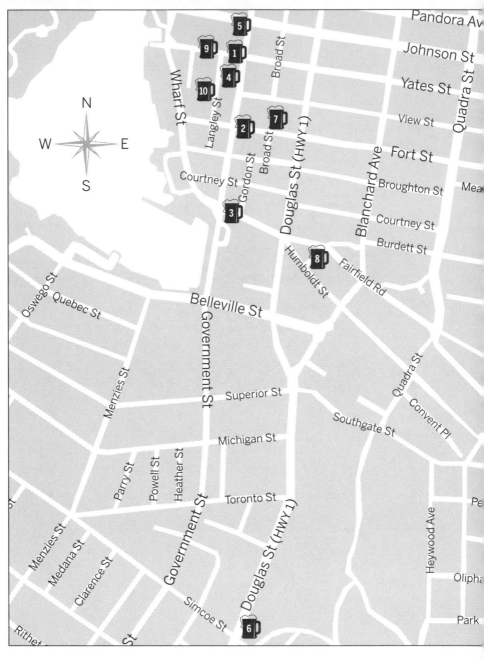

1. Adelphi Saloon
2. Brown Jug Saloon and Inn
3. Australian House
4. Confederate Saloon
5. Pony Saloon
6. Park Hotel
7. Bee Hive Hotel and Saloon
8. White Horse Hotel and Saloon
9. American Hotel
10. Garrick's Head Saloon

In the 1860s Johnson Street was located where the wooden sidewalk came to an abrupt end, and marked the northern edge of the city. It was perilous to walk there at night due to the poor lighting and the real possibility that one could take a nasty fall into the cavernous Johnson Street Ravine. Johnson Street was paradise to a drunk, as he had the choice of eighteen saloons and hotel bars to drink in. Most of the new saloons along this stretch of road attracted dubious characters who roamed the streets at all hours. Respectable citizens avoided the area. If they had business there they would go during daylight hours only, as it was just too dangerous at night.

Victorians enjoyed the benefits of a boom town. When the Fraser River Gold Rush subsided, a new strike in the Cariboo followed with similar frenzy. Closer to home, gold was discovered on the Leech River, approximately twenty miles north of Victoria. By 1864 Leechtown was an active boom town with a few dozen saloons and stores. The gold rush kept the saloons and hotel bars very busy, as most miners returned to Victoria in the winter to escape the harsh weather in the Cariboo. Those who could afford it stayed at one of the many hotels and spent their gold in the saloons. To attract customers, the hotel owners offered cut rates in the winter off-season. Governor Douglas declared Victoria a free port on January 1, 1860, as the sea port played an important role as a transportation link between

San Francisco and the goldfields of the Fraser and the Cariboo.

Victoria was a very muddy town in the winter and a dust bowl in the summer, but it was no longer called Fort Victoria as it rapidly outgrew its pioneer past. Between 1862 and 1864, the last remnants of the old Hudson's Bay fort were demolished. The City of Victoria was incorporated on August 2, 1862, with Thomas Harris as the first mayor. By 1865 the Crown Colony of Vancouver Island had its own flag approved by Queen Victoria, and Esquimalt was officially proclaimed the main base for the Royal Navy's Pacific Fleet by an Order-in-Council passed in London. The Royal Navy base gave an enormous boost to the local economy, providing a worldwide market for colonial goods.[2]

Smallpox and other diseases threatened Victorians, proving especially harsh on the Aboriginal population. Smallpox epidemics broke out in 1862, 1868, 1875–76, and 1888–89, and smallpox remained a viable threat until sophisticated medications were discovered to combat the disease and technology was developed to improve sanitary conditions throughout the city.[3] The smallpox outbreak of 1888 closed down the Burnes House on Bastion Street, and it never reopened as a hotel again.

The 1860s were a time of growth in the young colony, with gold fever helping to fuel excitement. This resulted in rambunctious behaviour at the numerous saloons and hotel bars in a town with such a small population. Some bars, like the Brown Jug Saloon, were quite tame; aside from the occasional fistfight, few problems occurred there. But other saloons, especially those notorious establishments found on Johnson Street, gained reputations as rough, wild, and downright dangerous, where frequent fighting became a spectator sport.

Sometimes those watching the fight would join in the melee and the brawl would spill out onto the street. Other times there would be betting on who would win the fight. The police were frequently summoned to break up fights, investigate petty thefts, and protect property. The most serious incidents were deadly, such as the discovery of a body under the floorboards of the Pony Saloon.

Locals knew where they liked to drink and which saloons to avoid. There are countless stories about the goings-on in the saloons at the rough edge of town, like the time young Jack McGinty entered the Albion Saloon while under the influence of liquor and called for a drink. He invited the barkeeper and a friend to join him, remarking, "You are the last men I shall ever drink with." After finishing the drink, he suddenly drew a jackknife from his pocket and plunged the blade into his left breast, making a fearful wound.[4]

Then there are the sordid adventures of people like Liverpool Jack, well known to the police as a desperate character, who managed to get himself into more fights than anyone in town. In one altercation in a Johnson Street saloon, Jack annoyed a stranger to the point where the angry man produced a revolver, pointed it at Jack, and threatened to blow his head off if Jack didn't back off. On another occasion Jack was found bloodied from a beating he had received after insulting a total stranger on the street. You could say that Jack was a slow learner. The bars were rife with riff-raff, and many of these unsavoury characters frequented the saloons along Johnson Street. A host of characters with colourful names like Washboard Mary, Old Black Jack, Dancing Bill, and Twelve-Foot Davis drank to excess in these saloons. They mixed in with the other regulars found in local saloons or out wandering the streets looking for their next drink.[5]

The saloon not only was a place to get a drink or start a fight, but also served as a "multipurpose community centre."[6] The saloon provided a spot where men could connect with one another and find work, get caught up with the latest news and gossip, follow the fortunes of their favourite sports teams, find accommodation, rub shoulders and bond, or simply rest in a dry, warm place. Most saloons offered free lunches to their drinking customers, and many bars featured various forms of entertainment, from rat races to musical acts. Billiards was a favourite pastime, and most saloons had billiard tables or a billiards room attached to their establishment. Saloons also provided a bathroom and, eventually, a telephone. Customers could usually find a bartender with a sympathetic ear, especially if they tipped him. Most bartenders cashed paycheques as a service for their regular customers, which proved convenient for workers who kept odd hours. Saloons operated like makeshift banks but without bankers' hours, as they were open twenty-four hours a day, seven days a week.

The saloon was mostly a male domain in which female customers were rare. "The small number of women willing to flaunt dominant bourgeois assumptions about the feminine ideal by enjoying the pleasures of booze in a public tavern faced harsh denunciations as 'bad mothers,' 'fallen women' or prostitutes."[7] Women did operate some establishments, and most saloons employed female cooks, servers, and entertainers.

Every saloon had an ample supply of hard liquor (spirits), which normally sold for twelve and a half cents a shot, and beer, which sold for five cents a mug. The saloons normally consisted of a spacious and ornate bar for patrons to lean on, spittoons to spit into, and a large painting over the bar, usually depicting a buxom lady or ladies in various states of undress for patrons to drool over. Indeed, the character and decor of each saloon were shaped by the character of its bartender or proprietor.

The American Civil War, 1861 to 1865, spilled over into Victoria. William Shapard's opening of the Confederate Saloon on Langley Street in the summer of 1863 annoyed the many Unionists in Victoria at that time. Immediately around the corner from the Confederate Saloon on Yates Street sat the American Saloon, with its own tall flagpole flying the Stars and Stripes. It was just a matter of time before the two antagonists would clash, in this case, over a stolen flag.

This chapter looks at the most notorious saloons and hotel bars in town, in some of which a handful of proprietors met their end by murder or suicide. Many of Victoria's long-term saloons and hotel bars opened in the 1860s and 1870s, and the following establishments provide a good sampling of what it was like to frequent the saloons on the rough edge of town.

ADELPHI SALOON
1861–1907

E. Chielovich and Samuel Melertich opened the Adelphi Saloon on the southwest corner of Government and (37–45) Yates Streets in 1861, and they operated it until January 1907. The earliest

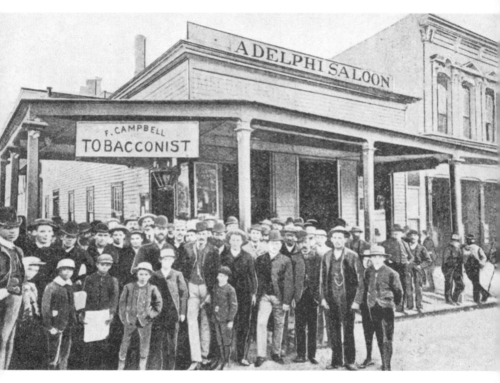

The Adelphi Saloon at Campbell's corner in the 1860s, where Victorians got their news.
IMAGE #B-04323 COURTESY OF THE ROYAL BC MUSEUM AND ARCHIVES

reference to the Adelphi Saloon comes from an advertisement in the *Colonist* in January 1862: "The racehorse Grey Arrow will be raffled for this evening at the Adelphi Saloon."[8]

The Adelphi was located next to Frank Campbell's tobacconist and general merchandise store at Government and Yates Streets. Campbell's Corner, as it was called, was the place to go for the latest in local and international news, complete with a bulletin board containing the day's top headlines.[9] Many of Campbell's customers would buy their newspaper and read it in the comfort of the Adelphi Saloon while enjoying a drink and a fine Cuban cigar, or smoking from a beautifully carved Meerschaum pipe, also purchased at Campbell's store. The Adelphi Saloon carried a large selection of fine brandies, wines, liquors, and ales. A separate games room was handsomely decorated with paintings. Engravings hung from the walls and featured "four of Phelan's patent combination cushions billiard tables."[10] Billiards and fifteen-ball pool were very popular, and most saloons provided their customers with at least one billiard table.

By 1870 the Adelphi Saloon was well known for its free and generous lunches. Clam chowder, oysters, chickens, and turkeys were served from 11 AM until 4 PM daily to anyone who bought a drink. Raffles were often held in which the prizes varied according to the season. Thanksgiving and Christmas saw plenty of large, plump turkeys won at the raffles, but prizes also included a horse and buggy and a very large gold nugget that weighed in excess of seventy-two ounces. Three hundred tickets sold at five dollars a pop for the gold nugget, which made a tidy profit for the house.

Raffles were legal, but gambling was not. Many saloons were raided over the years, but the Adelphi was not considered a common gaming house, especially when compared to the more unruly waterfront saloons along Wharf Street or the dive bars found along Johnson Street. A handful of gamblers were arrested in the back room of the Adelphi Saloon when it was learned that a game of studhorse poker was in progress. Another card game proved fatal for one of the participants when on December 15, 1872, Giovanni Zanoli, owner and captain of the schooner *Carolene*, sat down with a group of card players at the Adelphi and proceeded to lose a large sum of money at a game of rondo. Zanoli had bet and lost his last half-dollar when suddenly he clutched his chest and dropped violently to the floor, dead.[11]

Another incident occurred at the Adelphi when bartender J.H. Barnes was arrested for attempted murder in September 1884 after taking a few shots at a Mr. B. Wrede, who owned the Vancouver House. The shooting took place on Broad Street at three o'clock in the afternoon in a dispute over a debt that was owed. The two were heard shouting at each other, which turned into a pushing and shoving match, and that's when Barnes, face flushed red with anger, pulled a revolver out of his jacket and fired wildly at Wrede. Fortunately, he missed Wrede and the many innocent bystanders on the street at the time. The fracas was over a debt of three dollars. Barnes was held over for trial, with bail set at $500.[12]

The old wooden Adelphi Saloon closed in January 1907, and the liquor licence was transferred to the Atlantic Hotel at the corner of Johnson and Broad Streets. The empty building was purchased by the Northern Bank in February 1907, and extensive alterations were made over the following months. The Adelphi Block remained in business until May 1941, when it was demolished to make way for the main post office.

BROWN JUG SALOON AND INN
1861–1917

John D. Carroll opened the Brown Jug Saloon on the southeast corner of Fort and Government Streets on January 23, 1861. The land had previously been part of the Hudson's Bay Company apple orchard. Carroll immigrated to the United States from Ireland, then moved to Victoria in the late 1850s seeking opportunities during the gold rush. A grocer and liquor merchant, Carroll was operating a retail liquor store on Yates Street when he decided to go into the lucrative saloon business as well. On September 28, 1862, the first gas lamp in Victoria was illuminated in front of Carroll's liquor store.[13]

Carroll also began the first express wagon service that operated between Victoria and Esquimalt along the old forest trail that connected the two towns. Newspapers of the day described it as "an important public enterprise."[14] Carroll had also been involved in the Cariboo goldfields; he proudly displayed one of the fruits of his labour, "a fine nugget of gold," in a secure case in his store on Yates Street.

The Brown Jug was one of the more sophisticated and classy saloons at the time. The *Colonist* reported that "the interior is very tastefully and elegantly fitted up and attached to the main room is a reading room well stocked with reading material. It is a costly affair and we hope will prove profitable to its enterprising proprietor."[15] The striking bar was made of polished mahogany and, at fifty feet, was reputed to be the longest bar in the West. Bevelled mirrors, crystal glasses, and solid brass spittoons added

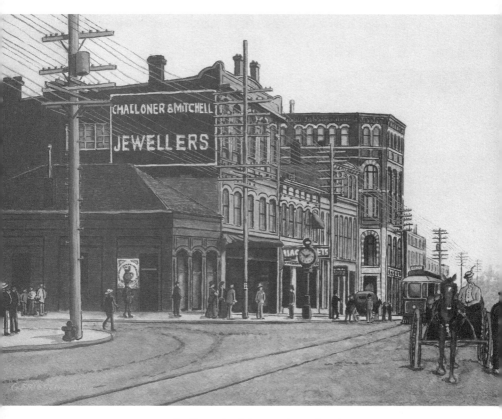

The Brown Jug Saloon on the southeast corner
of Fort and Government Streets, ca. 1909.
ARTWORK COURTESY OF GORDON FRIESEN, 2015

to the decor. No expense was spared in providing patrons with the very best.[16] Carroll did not tolerate rowdy behaviour in his saloon, and he trained his staff to toss the troublemakers.

Unfortunately, Carroll did not get the chance to enjoy his new saloon for long. He suffered from what was then called consumption; today we know it as tuberculosis. In July 1862 he left for San Francisco in hopes that the milder climate would aid in his recovery. His condition grew worse, however, and he died shortly after arriving in town, on July 14.[17]

Thomas Golden purchased the Brown Jug in the autumn of 1862. Golden was a member of the Odd Fellows, had owned and operated the Commercial Hotel, and had built the Three Star Saloon in the Cement Building located at the northeast corner of Wharf and Fort Streets (home of the Keg Restaurant at the time of writing). But fate proved to be very unkind to him.

Golden loved to gamble. By 1866 he found himself in financial trouble due to his inability to pay off his mounting gambling debts. He began selling his assets and continued to gamble, hoping that his luck would change, but his financial situation only grew worse. Finally, to recoup a portion of his losses, Golden considered leasing out his beloved Brown Jug for a term of one to five years, but he managed to keep the saloon.

By 1870 Golden had sold most of his properties, except his Three Star Saloon and the lucrative Brown Jug Saloon, as his financial situation continued to deteriorate. Left with no choice, on September 19, 1870, Golden sold the Brown Jug Saloon to his head bartender, Augustus Cecil Couves.[18] Golden then booked passage on a steamer to San Francisco. During the voyage he became so despondent over his debts and the loss of his saloons that he decided to commit suicide by jumping overboard. A passenger saw Golden jump into the sea and immediately informed a crew member. The ship came about and members of the crew rescued Golden. Shortly after declaring bankruptcy, Golden's mental health declined to the point where he was admitted to the California State Lunatic Asylum for treatment.[19] Thomas Golden was never heard from again.

The Brown Jug Saloon's new owner and operator, Augustus Cecil Couves, was born in Gravesend, County Kent, England. After arriving in Victoria he took on provisions to mine for gold, in which he had modest success. He returned to Victoria in 1866 and leased the Grotto Saloon on Government Street. In 1868 he left the Grotto and was hired as bartender at the Brown Jug Saloon. As the saloon's owner, Couves proved to be a sound entrepreneur, and the business thrived under his capable management right up until his death in July 1888. Couves's wife, Lucy, took over the business after her husband died and ran it successfully for three years before she sold it.

Like many of its competitors, the Brown Jug held raffles on a regular basis to attract customers and to raise money for local charities or creditable foundations. Some of the more interesting items raffled included "a magnificent rosewood piano," for which tickets sold for $2.50 each, and "four splendidly worked Berlin wool picture patterns" for only a dollar per ticket.[20] The Brown Jug occasionally displayed strange and unusual items for the amusement of patrons and the general public, such as "the monster chicken egg . . . the largest ever seen in the city,"[21] weighing in at six and a half ounces and measuring four and three-quarter inches long and four inches high.

The interior of the magnificent Brown Jug Saloon, ca. 1902.

Token issued by the Brown Jug from 1891 to 1899 when Mike Powers was the proprietor.
GLEN A. MOFFORD COLLECTION

Lucy Couves sold the Brown Jug to Michael Powers and William Croft in 1891, and by April of that year Powers had bought out his partner. Powers was born in Springfield, Massachusetts, in 1859, and he is first mentioned in the Victoria city directory in 1887 as proprietor of the Albion Saloon with his partner, John Remholdt Johnson.[22] Powers married Matilda Faulcner in October 1891, but his marriage proved all too brief when she died in April 1894. Powers didn't grieve long before he remarried in December of that year, to Nellie Burnell.

The Brown Jug happened to be built in a great location: the southeast corner of Fort and Government Streets, considered the heart of downtown Victoria in 1861 and featuring consistent walk-by traffic. Powers issued tokens for his business, with his name and the name of the Brown Jug on one side of the coin and "Good for one drink" on the flip side (see illustration above). A number of businesses issued such tokens for goods or services available only at their establishment.

After eight years as owner of the Brown Jug, Powers sold it in March 1899, then turned around and purchased the Garrick's Head Saloon on Bastion Street. But Powers would not live to see the end of the year, as he was murdered that October. The details of Powers's murder are revealed in the history of the Garrick's Head Saloon at the end of this chapter.

The Brown Jug continued to thrive. In the early 1900s its proprietors began producing their own beer, and by 1914 the owners expanded the business by adding a modest hotel next door to their famous saloon. The Brown Jug Hotel, later known as the Brown Jug Inn, looked as though its future would be very secure indeed, but a significant piece of legislation that became law in 1917 resulted in a very different outcome.

AUSTRALIAN HOUSE
1861–85

The Australian House was opened by John Wilson in February 1861 on the southeast corner of Humboldt and Government Streets. The hotel was a modest two-storey wooden building perched on stilts on the water side and connected to the north side of the James Bay Bridge. One advantage of having a hotel on the banks of James Bay was the wonderful fresh fish dinners, as reported in the *Colonist*: "A large codfish having been caught yesterday in the vicinity of James Bay, will be served up at the Australian House corner of Government and Humboldt Streets today."[23] With his new partner, Walter Miles, Wilson added nine small rooms on the top floor, two waterfront cottages in the back, and a saloon on the main floor. The hotel reopened on Saturday, May 16, 1863, after the considerable renovation.

The following year, Wilson and Miles sold the Australian

House to William Seeley. William Compton Smithfield Seeley and his wife, Ann, arrived in Victoria from England in 1859. Seeley built and repaired organs. In 1860 Seeley modified the barrel organ at the Christ Church Cathedral so that it could be played with a keyboard.[24] In 1869 Seeley salvaged the organ from the Christ Church Cathedral fire; although the organ was badly damaged, it was repaired and installed in his saloon "for the benefit of [the] musically inclined guests."[25]

On November 22, 1864, Ann Seeley gave birth to twin girls in the Seeleys' room above the saloon. The couple also had two boys, Thomas and James, but young Thomas died at the age of fifteen on November 2, 1873, from pneumonia. James would eventually inherit his father's hotel business.

An event took place inside the hotel on May 9, 1865, that nearly ended in disaster. William Seeley was going about his daily routine, cleaning the lamps in a room adjoining the bar, when a man entered the hotel. Seeley recognized him as Edmond Dillon, a local cabinetmaker who owned a shop a few doors down from the Australian House, and asked if he could be of service. Just as the words escaped Seeley's lips, Dillon pulled out a revolver and shot the hotelman, the ball entering above the navel and resting inside his left side. Seeley screamed, "You have murdered me!" and cried for help while reaching out to Dillon to prevent a second shot. Emanuel Bavare, an employee at the hotel, ran to Seeley's defence, and the two managed to wrestle the gun away from Dillon and subdue him until the police were summoned. Fortunately for Seeley, the wound was not life threatening, and the doctor removed the small ball.[26] The accused, Edmond Dillon, came up before Judge Cameron charged with assault with

The Australian House, southeast corner of Government and Humboldt Streets, 1863.
ARTWORK BY GORDON FRIESEN, 2015

a pistol with intent to kill. The unprovoked attack upon Seeley was reportedly not out of character for Dillon, who was subject to "violent paroxysms of rage, during which he assaults anyone he happens to meet."[27] Dillon was found not guilty due to insanity and was remanded to an insane asylum in San Francisco, where he died shortly thereafter in February 1866.[28]

Seeley survived the ordeal and continued to work diligently to make his hotel a success. In 1867 he added a "Water Cure Establishment" onto the south end of his hotel. For a small fee, customers wishing to enjoy the healing powers of seawater baths could immerse themselves in their choice of hot, cold, or tepid baths. Seeley also purchased a number of small boats for his patrons to use while staying at the hotel.

Apart from his hotel business, Seeley also purchased a soap factory located a few doors down from the hotel on the north side of James Bay. Crown Soap Works promised to provide "the best soap in the country," manufactured by W.C.S. Seeley & Co.

By December 1885 William Seeley had owned and operated his hotel for twenty-one years. Deciding it was time to retire, he asked his son James to take over the business. James Seeley, with his partner William G. Stevenson, paid for the licence for the Australian House and changed the name to the Arlington Hotel. Three years later, in December 1888, William Seeley died. Shortly after his death, son James leased the hotel under a new name, the Bay View Hotel. The hotel continued in business right up until 1904, when the City of Victoria purchased the hotel and the property to fill in James Bay and begin plans to build the Empress Hotel.

CONFEDERATE SALOON
1863–65

The American Civil War had been raging for two years when William Shapard and his partner, a man named Townsend, opened the Confederate Saloon on August 1, 1863. The partners leased a modest two-storey brick building on the north end of Langley near Yates Street in Victoria. Shapard had been working in Victoria since arriving with his wife and daughter from San Francisco in 1858. He followed the news from home closely and watched as the political turmoil rapidly deteriorated into civil war. Shapard decided that he could not leave to enlist while his family were left to fend for themselves in Victoria, so he quit his job, leased a small brick building on Langley Street, and opened a saloon where he could educate others about the virtues of the Southern cause.

Shapard was a Southern sympathizer and has been described as "keen, active and a good talker." [29] But he could also be argumentative, stubborn, and aggressive. The Confederate Saloon became quite popular for its generous free lunches, excellent rye whisky cocktails, and notorious gambling room, where Cariboo miners, sealers, sailors, refugees from the southern states, and local gamblers mixed, and where fortunes were won and lost. Prior to the outbreak of war, it didn't matter what state you came from, as most shared the common bond of being in a state of inebriation.

The saloon had an attached reading room that could also be used by clubs, organizations, and private companies to hold their meetings, like the shareholders meeting of the Muir Quartz Mining Company. A few of the empty rooms were used for gambling. Public gambling was illegal, but Shapard paid twenty dollars a week to the superintendent of police, Horace Smith, to turn a blind eye to the activities taking place at the Confederate Saloon. A handful of other saloons and hotel bars also paid bribes to Smith to keep their games from being raided until Smith was found out and faced corruption charges.[30]

One could easily find the Confederate Saloon, as Shapard had erected a tall flagpole out front on which he proudly flew the Stars and Bars, the flag of the Confederate States of America. Shapard dutifully hoisted the flag every morning at precisely nine o'clock and subsequently lowered the flag at sunset. It quickly became a ritual for him. He claimed the flag was on loan from the "Southern Ladies of Victoria," who stitched it in support of the Confederacy and to rally those with similar sympathy to his saloon.

Victoria was made up of a wide range of nationalities in the 1860s, but the majority of people came from the United States, Upper and Lower Canada, and Great Britain. Americans loyal to the Union were not impressed with Shapard or his Confederate Saloon. They were especially infuriated by the Confederate flag, which was like a red flag to a bull; they believed that something had to be done to quash this insult by Shapard and his rebel friends.

Tom Stratton was a loyal and passionate Unionist. He was a tall, thin man with a long black beard, which he continuously stroked while in conversation or when enjoying a beverage. Naturally Stratton and Shapard did not get along, as shown in this brief but heated encounter they had on Langley

Street: "One day," Stratton told Shapard, "if I could steal the Confederate flag I'd die a happy man." To which Shapard retorted, "If you should steal that flag you will die, but whether happy or not I cannot say. At any rate the flag, when you steal it, shall be your shroud."[31]

Stratton held a secret meeting with his friends and others loyal to the Union, and a plan was hatched. They would send a group of five or six men into the Confederate Saloon and pretend to be sympathetic to the Confederacy. They would catch Shapard and his friends off guard and steal the Confederate flag right from under Shapard's nose.

One early afternoon Stratton set his plan in motion. He sent five of his friends into the Confederate Saloon while Shapard was working behind the bar. They ordered a round and drank a toast to Jefferson Davis and the Confederacy. Shapard joined in the toast, as did the handful of Shapard's friends who were already in the saloon. The conspirators continued to buy Shapard and his friends drinks and to share news and swap stories about the war. One drink led to another, and as time wore on Shapard became quite relaxed with the new crowd, who blended in with other regulars in the bar. Shapard became so intoxicated that he forgot about lowering the flag at sunset and instead fell asleep as the next bartender came on shift. Meanwhile, hidden by the darkness of night, one of Stratton's men slipped outside and quickly lowered the flag, which he then hid in his jacket.

When Shapard woke the next day, and as his wits slowly returned, he walked out to the front of his saloon and found that his flag was not there. It didn't take long for him to realize that he had been duped and that the flag had been stolen.

He then heard a rumour that Stratton had been overheard boasting about stealing the flag. An infuriated Shapard swore vengeance. Shapard found Stratton sitting at Ringo's Restaurant, not far from the Confederate Saloon. "You stole my flag," Shapard foamed. A fight ensued and blows were exchanged, and it quickly became an all-out brawl. When it finally ended, the two combatants were bruised and bloodied and Stratton's long black beard was in Shapard's left hand, pulled right off of his chin during the altercation.

The flag was never found, but it was revealed after the war that it had been turned over to the American embassy and sent to Washington, DC. Shapard left for San Francisco with his family in about December 1865 or shortly thereafter. The two-storey brick building that once housed the Confederate Saloon became a post office.

I never found out if Tom Stratton could ever grow a full beard again.

PONY SALOON
1863–70

Of all the unsolved murder mysteries that occurred during these times, the most captivating and certainly the most disturbing occurred at the Pony Saloon sometime between 1862 and 1870. The Pony Saloon, previously known as the Highland Mary Saloon (1862) was located at (100–130) 1324 Government Street near Johnson Street, with Charles Hounslow as proprietor.

Advertisement for the Pony Saloon, *British Colonist.*

Pioneer Victoria was a rough place in the 1860s, and this was especially true along Johnson and Government Streets, where most of the new saloons could be found. It proved to be particularly rough at night. The saloons were full most evenings, especially when the sailors were in town on leave. A good time was had by all—well, almost all—but it wasn't long before the criminal element saw an opportunity to make some fast money. An unsuspecting sailor or gold miner, usually quite inebriated, provided an easy mark. When alone in an alley, staggering to the next saloon, the innocent victim would be approached from behind and struck on the head with a heavy object, just hard enough to knock him out. He would wake with a sore head and find that his pockets had been picked and all his cash and usually his watch and other valuables stolen. But one victim did not wake up the next day. His attackers accidentally applied too much force when cracking him over the head, and to their dismay, the victim died from the assault. The body was disposed of in a most unusual and undignified manner, and the incident was kept quiet for years.

The Pony Saloon saw a change in proprietors in 1865 when Hounslow sold to an American, Phillip Smith. Smith and his "red-headed woman friend" loved to entertain; she would sing and dance and Smith would host high-stakes poker games that would last well into the following day.[32] The Pony Saloon fit in perfectly with the rowdy reputation of that area of town. Smith ran the Pony Saloon for the next five years, selling to George Mason in December 1870.[33] Mason changed the name of the saloon to the Omineca Saloon. Meanwhile, Smith and his family moved to San Francisco in December 1870 aboard the *Pelican*. Smith was in very poor health, and once there he became violently insane.[34] Was his condition brought on by tremendous guilt?

By the mid-1880s most of the wooden buildings in town were being torn down and replaced with brick buildings. A bylaw was passed that banned building with wood over a certain height, so brick was the best alternative. The Omineca, the old Pony Saloon, was one of the establishments being renovated from wood to brick. During the demolition a worker was using a crowbar to pry up the floorboards in the back of the old saloon when he "let it fall with an exclamation of horror. His fellow-workmen crowded about the spot as he raised a plank exposing to view a human skull with the upper jaw minus three teeth, and the lower jaw missing. The remainder of the planking was quickly torn up and more human remains were found."[35]

Work immediately came to a halt once the gruesome discovery was made. Doctor Trimble examined the remains and concluded that they were those of a "white man," and he speculated that the jaw of this person had been split by violence. The victim was most likely murdered for his money. This revelation didn't come as a shock to some of the city's older residents who recalled that the saloon had a reputation for "horrible bacchanalian orgies in which dissolute men and women joined."[36] Many poor miners were robbed of their hard-earned cash and tumbled into the street penniless. But who had committed this ghastly murder? Was it Phil Smith? If he wasn't the murderer, had he had a hand in hiding the body in the back room of his saloon? Or was it one of the Pony Saloon's regular patrons who had needed some quick money to remain at the gambling table? It was later revealed that a regular gambler at the saloon had left suddenly in 1863 accompanied by the red-haired lady, and the pair had never been seen again. Could they have had something to do with the murder?

An inquest into the death of the victim resulted in more questions than answers, and the case remains unsolved to this day, another cold-case mystery that took place on the rough edge of town.

PARK HOTEL
1864–86

The aptly named Park Hotel opened on September 6, 1864, on the edge of Beacon Hill Park at the northeast corner of Simcoe and Catherine (now Douglas) Streets in James Bay. The hotel owners, appropriately named William and Henrietta Lush, purchased an acre of land from Richard Carr, who had bought several acres from the Hudson's Bay Company farm the year before, where he built his home. Carr had a verbal agreement with the Lushes that he would sell them an acre of his property if they agreed not to build a hotel; they agreed, shook hands, then built the Park Hotel,[37] perhaps not a great way to ingratiate themselves to the neighbours or to Mr. Carr. Carr reacted by building a high fence between the properties, all the while regretting the sale and concerned about the noise and traffic that a hotel with a bar might bring. Carr had good reason to worry.

William and Henrietta (née Immel) were married on February 11, 1863. After purchasing the property from Mr. Carr, they applied for a liquor licence in June 1864. There was some opposition at licensing court, as most of the members of the board were against the Lushes receiving a liquor licence, stating that a hotel was neither wanted nor desirable. The licence was initially refused. The Lushes applied again for a licence at the next sitting of the licensing board. This time William came armed with a petition signed by many of his neighbours who were in favour of his application. It was granted. Needless to say, Mr. Carr's name was not on the petition.

With the hotel completed and liquor licence approved, the Park Hotel quickly gained a reputation as a notorious watering hole. As Emily Carr, daughter of Richard Carr and future celebrated writer and artist, wrote, "Hacks filled with tipsy sailors and noisy ladies drove past our house going to the Park Hotel in the daytime and at night. It hurt Father right up till he was seventy years old when he died."[38] The Lushes enjoyed their drinking parties, holding free balls at their hotel on a regular

The Lushes' Park Hotel, corner of Douglas and Simcoe Streets in James Bay.
IMAGE #A-06625 COURTESY OF THE ROYAL BC MUSEUM AND ARCHIVES

basis and supplying picnic dinners and drinks for those who wished to enjoy the park. They offered guests a long table in the dining room complete with "all the delicacies of the season, plus bumpers of champagne."[39]

William Lush was an argumentative, stubborn Irishman who never backed down from a fight, but in the end he was a dedicated hotelman. He came to Victoria in 1858 from California and followed the other fortune seekers to the Fraser River goldfields. He then returned to Victoria to stay. Lush's wife, Henrietta, had experience operating the successful Metropolitan Lodging House on Yates Street before she married William.[40] Together they planned to build a hotel of their own, and when the opportunity came along in 1864, nothing would stand in their way.

The Lushes enjoyed their hotel through the 1860s and into the early 1870s. There was no competition on that side of town; the closest bar was far across the park near Clover Point on Dallas Road, where Henley's Hotel had opened in 1864. But by 1875 the party ended for Mr. Lush.

William Lush was no stranger to the courts. He had been in trouble on a number of occasions, due in part to his stubborn nature and abrasive attitude, and had faced the judge numerous times in the past. On Tuesday, January 26, 1875, Lush found himself once more before a judge. The charge this time was for selling liquor to an Aboriginal person. Lush conducted his own defence, but in the end he was found guilty as charged. He was sentenced to pay a fine of $150 plus court costs or spend three months in jail. Lush requested time to raise the money; the request was granted provided he obtain the funds to pay the fine by three o'clock that day.

Lush found it difficult to collect enough money to pay the fine, but he was determined he would not end up in prison. He began drinking. Lush entered the Brown Jug Saloon on Government Street, where he had a drink with a friend before taking his leave with a small quantity of whisky. When Lush did not show up in court at the appointed time, a warrant was issued for his arrest. He was found later that day inside the Ten Pin Alley, a business he owned but was forced to close. Lush lay dead on the floor with a small bottle beside him. It was later determined that he had died by committing suicide; he had swallowed a lethal dose of strychnine and died a rather gruesome and violent death.[41]

Henrietta continued the business as the sole proprietor until she sold the hotel to Samuel Evans in 1879. By 1886 the hotel was renamed the Colonist Hotel. In 1891 new owner Catherine Hotz replaced the aging hotel with a brick structure equipped with electric lights and two tennis courts.[42] The Colonist Hotel lasted until 1912, when the liquor licence was transferred to the new James Bay Hotel on Government Street. The old Colonist Hotel became a tea room until it was demolished in 1924.

BEE HIVE HOTEL AND SALOON
1864–1908

Mrs. F.A. Byrnes opened the Bee Hive Hotel on the northeast corner of 1111 Broad and (48) 630 Fort Streets in the spring of

1864. The hotel, formerly a two-storey farmhouse, consisted of ten rooms and a barroom with an adjoining billiards room. A glass case containing a valuable selection of stuffed Vancouver Island birds was on display in the lobby. The Bee Hive also provided a room for clubs and societies, such as the Amateur Theatre Group of Victoria, to hold their meetings. Guests could enjoy a meal in the small restaurant in the hotel, where oysters were the specialty of the house.[43] Two additional single-storey brick buildings on the property housed the saloon and the liquor store.

Mrs. Byrnes sold the hotel and saloon to Edward R. Thomas in 1864—the same year she opened it. Thomas and his bartender Charles Pagden ran the Bee Hive until 1869, when Captain James Cooper bought the place. Captain Cooper, previously the Lloyds agent in Victoria, ran the hotel for a short time, but when he wanted to sell and had trouble finding a buyer, he decided to close the establishment. The Bee Hive was vacant until 1872, when it was finally sold; John Beecroft was the new owner. The Bee Hive went through several more owners until 1884, when Mathew Francis kept the hotel business but sold off the saloon and liquor store.

It was around this time that the famous artist Emily Carr, while a young girl in the 1880s, was visiting her sister in downtown Victoria and was saved from being trampled by a herd of cattle that rushed down Fort Street by the quick actions of an employee of the Bee Hive Saloon. He grabbed Emily off of the street and out of danger, dragging her inside the saloon. As her eyes got accustomed to the dark of the saloon, Carr described what she saw:

I looked around the Saloon. Shiny taps were beside me and behind the long counter-bar ran shelves full of bottles and sparkling glasses; behind them again was a looking-glass so that it seemed to be twice as many bottles and twice as many glasses as there were . . . In the back half of the saloon were barrels and small wooden tables; chairs with round backs stood about the floor with their legs sunk in sawdust; bright brass spittoons were everywhere. The saloon was full of the smell of beer and sawdust.[44]

Thanks to Carr's descriptive story, we have a better idea of what the Bee Hive Saloon looked and smelled like in the early to mid 1880s. Indeed, many of the working-class saloons were quite similar.

The Bee Hive Saloon continued in business with a different owner approximately every couple of years. One owner, James S. Cowie, who was proprietor from 1884 to 1891, was attacked by Special Constable John McDonald. It appears that McDonald, while off duty and quite inebriated, believed he heard Cowie make a disparaging remark about him. McDonald demanded Cowie take it back and apologize, but a puzzled Cowie ignored the constable. That's when McDonald pulled out his concealed revolver and threatened to shoot the saloon owner. Fortunately, a friend of McDonald's was present and took the gun away from him. McDonald was later found guilty of common assault and sentenced to one year of hard labour.[45]

In the summer of 1885 the Beehive Saloon displayed a most unusual attraction. Dubbed the Metchosin Monster, the grisly attraction consisted of an immense, petrified man—minus his arms and legs—"discovered" on the Gilbert farm in Happy Valley. "For 25 cents Victorians could view his grey form in a coffin-like box and hear of farmer Gilbert's amazing story."[46] Captain A.E. McCallum was very intrigued by the discovery, and after paying his twenty-five cents to view the thing, he offered Mr. Dubois, who represented Gilbert, the sum of £300 (around $1,500) to purchase it. Dubois accepted, and Captain McCallum was the new owner of the petrified giant. He planned to exhibit the giant for a time, make his money back plus a tidy sum for himself, then donate it to the British Museum.

Captain McCallum's dream of making a fortune quickly turned into a nightmare when he learned that customs had seized it—after he had paid for it—for suspected undervaluation. It seems that a customs agent had recently allowed the vaguely humanoid figure into Victoria from San Francisco and that the party entering with the object had claimed it to be a large piece of limestone, for which they were required to pay one dollar. The strange case went to court, as McCallum was convinced that the petrified figure was genuine, in spite of police suspicions and the world-renowned geologist Dr. George M. Dawson stating that it was a very artistic forgery.

The case was heard on January 7, 1886. A Happy Valley woman testified that she had heard and watched some men bury the object in farmer Gilbert's field some months back and that the whole thing was an elaborate hoax.[47]

On March 12, 1908, Mrs. Anna Burns, the last owner of the Bee Hive Saloon, sold the liquor licence to A.R. Macdonald, who successfully transferred the licence to the Alberta Saloon on Broad Street.

WHITE HORSE HOTEL AND SALOON
1865-1922

The two-storey brick White Horse Tavern was opened on
the northeast corner of McClure and Humboldt Streets on
November 4, 1865, by partners named Ball and Mason. The
elegant yet simple building was designed by Richard Lewis
(1824–75), known for designing some of the most impressive
commercial structures in colonial Victoria. Among the buildings Lewis designed that survive today are most of those found
along the east side of Wharf Street from Fort Street north to
Bastion Square, known as Commercial Row; a brick hospital
on Collinson Street for the Sisters of St. Ann; two single-storey
brick stores in the Italianate style for saloon owner Thomas
Golden; and an additional floor on top of the Cement Building
at the corner of Fort and Wharf Streets, which was leased out to
the Odd Fellows organization.[48]

William Reid leased and operated the White Horse until he
died in 1881; his son, James, purchased the lease. Meanwhile,
the ownership of the hotel changed hands in April 1867 when
Ball and Mason sold to J. Adair.

The close proximity of the White Horse to the Parliament
Buildings made it a popular destination for members of the
legislative assembly, who dropped in for a discreet drink. One of
the advantages of the hotel was its location off the beaten path
and away from the noise and smells of downtown Victoria.

That's not to say there were no significant incidents at the
White Horse Hotel—specifically, in the hotel bar. Of special note

is the fracas that took place in the cabins beside the White Horse Hotel in 1884. John "Dutch Charley" Malmborg, a seafaring man living in one of the cabins, was attacked with an axe by his neighbour Henry Knight. Dutch Charley received two serious blows, one to the head and the other to his chest, exposing his left lung. Dr. Helmcken attended to his wounds in the White Horse Saloon. Dutch Charley was taken to the Royal Hospital, and though he was not expected to survive, he prevailed. After a brief chase, Knight was arrested and charged with attempted murder.[49]

A number of thefts occurred at the White Horse through the years. A sailor was charged with stealing $100 worth of jewellery from the hotel. He pleaded guilty to the charge, but the judge was not impressed when the sailor claimed he was too drunk to be held responsible for his actions. The judge sentenced him to ten days in jail. Another theft took place in the hotel bar while the bartender was tending to a customer. It was alleged that Peter McLaughlin took the opportunity to open the till and steal thirty-five dollars, but the judge threw out the case for lack of evidence.

A disturbing event took place inside the bar of the White Horse when long-time regular and well-known barber George North was enjoying his customary pint of beer. Suddenly he clutched his chest and fell to the floor, dead, from a heart attack.[50] Perhaps his demise was brought on by the news that the price of a mug of beer at the White Horse had dropped from ten cents to five cents a mug.

A minor scandal—though it received considerable press— occurred in the White Horse Saloon in June 1909. Proprietors Neil Hansen and Hans Keisow and another male were entertaining two young local women in the back of the saloon after closing time. Licence Inspector Hanley noted that "at 12:30 a.m. on [the]

The White Horse Hotel and Saloon, northeast corner of Humboldt and Blanshard Streets.
IMAGE #F-00015 COURTESY OF THE ROYAL BC MUSEUM AND ARCHIVES

27th, two young women, daughters of respectable parents, and a male companion were discovered in the rear of the saloon."[51] The owners faced two charges: selling liquor during prohibited hours and allowing females to frequent the premises during prohibited hours. After the case was deliberated, the owners were found guilty on both charges. Mayor Hall, chairman of the Board of Licensing Commissioners, suspended their liquor licence for thirty days and added, "I regret that the board does not have the authority to impose the lash for men who entice young girls into saloons."[52]

In 1913 the owners of the White Horse Hotel hired architect J.C.M. Keith to design an addition to the hotel. The reputable Parfitt Brothers Construction Company won the contract to build the extension at the cost of approximately $18,000.[53]

In October 1917, Prohibition closed the popular hotel bar, but the White Horse Hotel continued in business until 1922. A new owner changed the hotel rooms to apartments, operating the business as the Humboldt Apartments from 1923 to 1935. In 1936 the name changed again to the Glen Court Hotel Rooms. The Sisters of St. Ann purchased the building and had it demolished in October 1959 to make way for a parking lot for St. Joseph's Hospital.

AMERICAN HOTEL
1867–96

In 1867 Thomas (Tommy) J. Burnes purchased the American Hotel located on the south side of (15) 535 Yates Street near

Commercial Alley. The hotel was a three-storey wood structure containing thirty-two rooms with a saloon on the ground floor. Built in 1859, the hotel was easy to locate, as it was fronted by a very tall flagpole flying the Stars and Stripes. It's not surprising that there was an American Hotel in Victoria, as Americans made up a significant part of the population of the city in the 1860s. "The Fourth of July was celebrated with the same enthusiasm as the Queen's birthday on May 24th."[54]

Tommy Burnes was born in Dublin, Ireland. He immigrated to the United States and eventually landed in San Francisco in 1854, where he got a job in the post office. Burnes then joined the thousands of men who came to Victoria during the stampede for gold in 1858, but instead of going to the mainland to try his luck mining gold, he stayed in Victoria, where he found a secure job working as a customs agent. By 1862 Burnes had tried his hand at the saloon business by buying the Pioneer Saloon at Johnson Street and Oriental Alley.[55] He worked hard in his saloon until he had saved enough money to pay passage for his fiancée, who was living in New York City at the time, to come to Victoria. Miss Kate McCloy was one of 1,700 passengers who left New York on April 1, 1862, aboard a steamer bound for San Francisco. The journey took nine days from New York through the Panama Canal and north along the coast to San Francisco. The trip was considered quite dangerous, as the American Civil War was in its second year. An American gunboat was dispatched for the protection of the passengers and crew.[56] Burnes and McCloy married in May 1862 shortly after she arrived safely in Victoria. Through their long and happy marriage, they had eight children, of which four survived to go on and have successful careers.

Tommy Burnes and friends standing outside his American Hotel on Yates Street.
IMAGE #F-00037 COURTESY OF THE ROYAL BC MUSEUM AND ARCHIVES

By 1872 the American Hotel had a popular saloon, a thirty-two-room hotel, and a retail wine and spirit department; the last was leased out to John Feight. February 22, 1872, marked Washington's birthday, and the hotel was decorated inside and out to honour the first president of the United States. Flags flew from the pole on top of the hotel and on the tall pole out front. Windy conditions damaged the flag on top of the hotel, but Burnes "climbed up onto the roof like an acrobat and repaired it."[57]

Like most saloons and hotel bars, the American Hotel held its fair share of raffles. Other forms of entertainment included performances by a vaudeville troupe in the bar. For a mere ten dollars, one could also purchase a dozen "famous Bremmer Foul [sic] Eggs at the American Hotel."[58]

In 1886 Burnes decided to build another hotel on Bastion Street, not too far from his American Hotel. The handsome three-storey brick Burnes House opened as "one of Victoria's earliest luxury hotels to serve successful gold miners and English remittance men."[59] After twenty-three years in business, Tommy Burnes sold the American Hotel to George Shea in September 1890. Although he didn't need the money, Burnes did not retire, instead returning to his previous job working for the customs agency.

On June 15, 1893, an explosion took place in the back of the bar of the American Hotel. Apparently an oil lamp had somehow caught on fire, and the resulting explosion and fire caused $4,000 worth of damage.[60] Dungeon and Brice, the lessees of the hotel, had $2,200 in insurance on the building, and they decided to rebuild in brick rather than repair the damage.

Another significant event occurred at the American Hotel on October 11, 1895. By this time the hotel had taken on boarders, and within a year the hotel would close and become a rooming house. But for the time being, Mrs. May Fox managed the hotel. Three brothers, on leave from their jobs as sealers, had been drinking most of the day when they arrived at the American Hotel. They were talking and laughing with a number of young women at the hotel when one of the brothers, William Farrell, foolishly took out a revolver and pretended to shoot one of the ladies. The gun did not go off and they all had a good laugh. But when Farrell pointed his revolver at Georgie Douglas a second time and pulled the trigger, the gun did go off, and the bullet struck Miss Douglas in the leg above the knee. City Detective Perdue was patrolling the area and was quickly summoned. He arrested all three brothers and contacted the hospital to make arrangements for the wounded Douglas. Farrell was booked for malicious wounding as it appeared that Douglas might lose her leg.[61]

A month after the shooting, Georgie Douglas had not recovered sufficiently to testify and the trial was postponed until June 17, 1896. William Farrell had been in custody since the shooting and had all that time to ponder and regret his foolish actions. The other two Farrell brothers had been set free shortly after the incident but were subpoenaed to testify at the trial. On June 20, 1896, Farrell was found guilty of accidentally wounding Miss Georgie Douglas. Justice Drake sentenced Farrell to time served plus four months.[62] I never did find out if Miss Douglas kept her leg.

Five proprietors came and went after Burnes sold the American Hotel, until the last owner, Robert Hamilton, closed the place in 1896. The old hotel became a rooming house, and in 1900 it was torn down and replaced by the building that occupies the space today.

GARRICK'S HEAD SALOON
1868–1913

The Garrick's Head Saloon was established on January 1, 1868, at (23) 547 Bastion Street by Thomas Chadwick. Chadwick was an energetic man; while he operated the Garrick's Head he was also proprietor of the International Hotel on the southeast corner of Yates and Douglas Streets from 1862 to 1883, and he bought the Blue Post Saloon at Johnson and Douglas Streets after selling the Garrick's Head Saloon in 1871. A group of Chadwick supporters put his name forward for the local elections, and Chadwick was elected representative for the Johnson Street Ward. Chadwick turned the post down, saying he was too busy with his saloon and hotel operations.[63]

In 1871 John Wilson purchased the Garrick's Head Saloon from Chadwick, running it until 1883, longer than any other proprietor. Like Chadwick before him, Wilson was an experienced bartender and saloon owner, having worked at the Bank Exchange and Australian House Saloons. While running the Garrick's Head Wilson also purchased the Fountain Saloon on Douglas Street at Yates.

Various organizations used a room off the Garrick's Head barroom for their meetings. The Number 2 Company of the Victoria Militia met there to plan strategy for their upcoming football game against the navy team. The Garrick's Head Saloon also held raffles. Tickets sold for three dollars, giving ticket holders a chance to win a twenty-eight-foot boat complete with a boathouse to keep it in. The total package was worth the tidy sum of $500.[64]

Wilson was always looking to improve his business, and when the opportunity arose for expansion he jumped at the chance. A few of the wooden buildings next door to the Garrick's Head at the corner of Government and Bastion Streets were being replaced with a new large brick building. Wilson purchased the unfinished building, and in January 1879 he moved his saloon to the new location.[65] Wilson finally had enough space to add a billiards room and an enlarged meeting room. The saloon had now moved to the corner of the block, allowing for better visibility for potential drop-in customers.

After Wilson sold the Garrick's Head in 1883 a succession of owners came and went, including E.W. Spencer (pictured on p. 85), and it was business as usual until Mike Powers, late of the Brown Jug, purchased the saloon on June 14, 1899. Powers came from Springfield, Massachusetts, and had gained his experience in the saloon business when he partnered with John Remholdt Johnson at the Albion Saloon from 1886 to 1890. He then bought the Brown Jug Saloon, which he owned from 1891 until April 1899. Powers looked forward to improving his new saloon, but fate had other plans.

After closing up the Garrick's Head one night, Powers walked to his home on Fort Street. It was approximately three o'clock in the morning when Powers arrived at the front gate to his house. He heard a noise behind him, and as he turned to see who it was, he was struck with a heavy object and knocked off his feet. The object was later identified as a sack filled with sand. Stunned and bleeding on the ground, Powers tried to defend himself from two assailants who began kicking him mercilessly. Powers yelled for help, "Oh Edna, Edna, bring me my gun!" The attackers ran off

The Garrick's Head Saloon, 547 Bastion Street, ca. 1889. From left to right:
William McNiffe, proprietor of the Grotto Saloon on Government Street,
E.W. Spencer, proprietor of the Garrick's Head, and S. Green.
IMAGE #A-04661 COURTESY OF THE ROYAL BC MUSEUM AND ARCHIVES

when the front door opened and a person with a lighted lamp called out.[66]

Edna Rowen had been the housekeeper for Mike Powers since his separation two years earlier from his wife, Nellie, who had moved to the mainland to be with her family. Powers and Rowen had begun a romance and had plans to marry once his divorce from his first wife was finalized. The two assailants were thought to be a man and a woman dressed as a man. Nellie Powers was not suspected, as she was on the mainland at the time of the assault on her estranged husband.

Initially Powers did not appear to have sustained life-threatening injuries, but his condition worsened over the next few days to the point where he was admitted to Jubilee Hospital. On Thursday afternoon, five days after he was attacked, Powers succumbed to his injuries. The coroner's inquest determined that the cause of Powers's death was peritonitis, produced by a rupture of the intestine from the kicks he had received while on the ground.[67] It was also determined that robbery was not the motive, as Powers still had the seventy dollars he had left the saloon with.

Meanwhile, the staff and regular customers of the Garrick's Head toasted the memory of their employer and friend and the bar was kept open as per usual. A $500 reward was offered for information leading to an arrest, but the case was never solved. A notice was printed in the newspaper on October 18 asking for tenders to purchase the licence and goods of the Garrick's Head Saloon. Harry E. Morton bought the Garrick's Head from the estate of Michael Powers.

Though many owners came and went (including E.W. Spencer, seen in the image on page 85), the last proprietor of the Garrick's

Head was Arthur Knowles Vaughan, who operated the saloon from 1909 until it closed in 1913. In 1911 all saloon owners in British Columbia were warned that stand-alone saloons would no longer be licensed as of January 1914.[68] Saloon owners had three years to add a hotel or face closure. Mr. Vaughan hoped that he could secure additional space for a small attached hotel, but by July 1913 his plans had fallen through. The Garrick's Head Saloon was forced to close in December 1913.[69]

The frenzy of activity that began in 1858 with the Fraser River Gold Rush continued through the 1860s, fuelled further when gold was discovered in the Cariboo and on the Leech River on Vancouver Island. A series of economic booms and busts took place from late 1864 through the 1870s. While Victoria experienced a gradual growth in local businesses, the number of new saloons and hotel bars exploded to eighty-five licensed establishments—not counting the unlicensed saloons. In this chapter we focused on the most notorious working-class bars and saloons; in stark contrast, in Chapter Three we will discover the best hotels that operated in the city from the 1860s through the 1910s.

CHAPTER THREE

STRICTLY FIRST-CLASS

A man hath no better thing under the sun, than to
eat, and to drink, and to be merry.

—Ecclesiastes 8:15 [1]

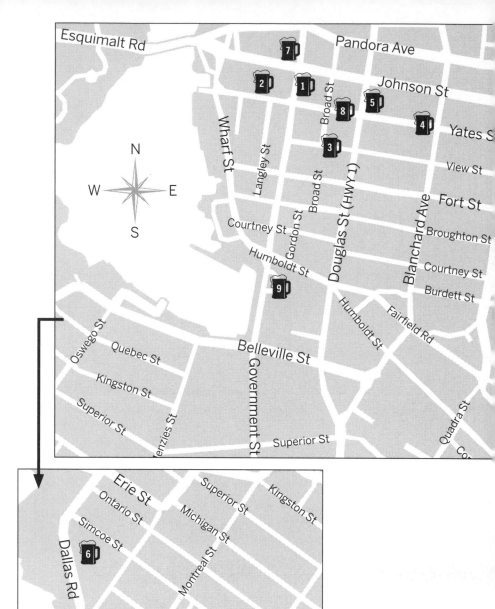

1. St. Nicholas Hotel
2. Oriental Hotel
3. Driard Hotel
4. Dominion Hotel
5. Clarence Hotel
6. Dallas Hotel
7. Victoria Hotel (III)
8. King Edward Hotel
9. Empress Hotel

B eing a port city and later the capital of British Columbia, Victoria required first-class hotels. From 1860 to 1920 the travelling public could choose from an increasing variety of first-class establishments, and as technology improved, these palatial hotels offered a whole new level of sophistication, luxury, and superb service. When a traveller arrived at the wharf or train station, they were met by the hotel carriage, their bags were picked up, and they were whisked away to one of the finest hotels on the west coast of North America.

Sometimes the hotel bar played a role in attracting tourists to a particular hotel. While temperance hotels existed and did a fair business, the high-class hotels, with their spacious billiards rooms and long mahogany bars, attracted the bulk of travellers. Men of means flocked to these hotel bars to take pleasure in a cigar, enjoy a favourite beverage, and read a newspaper in an atmosphere of quiet opulence. The rich drank spirits and wines on a regular basis, the most popular after-dinner drink being port.[2]

While most of the first-class hotels were built with the intention of serving wealthy guests, a handful of others developed gradually over time. Hotels like the Oriental Hotel, the Dominion Hotel, and the Driard House all had modest beginnings and increasingly improved to the point of becoming strictly first-class.

Early first-class hotels of the 1860s and 1870s included

the St. Nicholas Hotel, the Colonial Hotel, and the Hotel de France, all on Government Street; the Fashion Hotel on Yates Street; and the Pacific Telegraph Hotel on Store Street. In the 1880s came the Burnes House on Bastion Street, the Clarence Hotel on Douglas Street, the Delmonico Hotel—which changed its name from the St. Nicholas—and the Pritchard House on Yates Street. By the 1890s and "prior to the building of the Empress Hotel in 1908, a visitor to Victoria seeking a superior hotel in town would undoubtedly have chosen one of the big four—the Victoria, the Dallas, the Mount Baker in Oak Bay, or the Driard House."[3]

This chapter looks at some of these first-class establishments of Victoria, beginning in the 1860s and continuing through to 1908, when the most magnificent hotel of them all opened on the waterfront. We will also explore the bar or bars that each of these exceptional hotels provided for their guests and learn what it was like for the affluent tourist who travelled strictly first-class.

ST. NICHOLAS HOTEL
1862–88

The beautiful three-storey brick St. Nicholas Hotel was opened at (107–109) Government Street just north of Yates in November 1862 by Matthiessen and Company, who hired H.F. Heisterman as proprietor. The luxury hotel opened with a strikingly decorated restaurant, a first-rate bar, a ladies' ordinary, and "the Exchange" reading room. A large plush billiards room opened in December.

The St. Nicholas Hotel

NOTICE TO TRAVELERS.

THE GREATER PORTION

OF

THIS FINE THREE STORY

BRICK HOTEL

Is now ready for the accommodation of

THE TRAVELING PUBLIC.

no 29 lw

Advertisement for the St. Nicholas Hotel, *British Colonist*.

It was located just off the hotel bar and was managed by Quarles & Company, Jewellers.[4]

The Victoria Exchange Reading and News Room was essentially a private club within the hotel where members paid to access newspapers and magazines from around the world. The club also featured a games room (chess was a popular game at the time). The membership rates were twenty-five cents per day, three dollars per month, or twenty-four dollars per year.[5]

The St. Nicholas Hotel played a small part in the American Civil War. There was a fairly large group of Southerners and Southern sympathizers in Victoria. Two brothers from Alabama, John and Oliver Jeffreys, rented rooms at the St. Nicholas, where they gathered to drink a toast to Jefferson Davis and celebrate early Confederate victories. The Jeffreys brothers shared a scheme they had just come up with while enjoying a few beers in the St. Nicholas Bar and in the Confederate Saloon just a few blocks away on Langley Street. After much discussion, which included table thumping, grandstanding, and consuming a great quantity of beer, a plot was hatched in which the English ship *Thames* would be purchased and modified into a privateer. The ship would be used to attack American gold shipments out of San Francisco and deliver the stolen gold to the Confederate cause.[6] But after months of trying to raise enough money to buy the ship, they gave up and devised an alternative plan.

Instead of buying a ship, they would seize one. The side-wheel steamer USS *Shubrick* was the target of their scheme, but attempts to seize the ship fell apart due to disorganization, lack of leadership, and just plain incompetence. "Activities there were, although not of an incendiary nature. Southerners sat around the bar in the St. Nicholas Hotel in Victoria to drink beer and appollinairs [*sic*] water and to concoct plots against the North, but nothing came of their ruminations."[7] Allen Francis at the American consulate was aware of the activities of these Southern sympathizers at all times and took the necessary steps to thwart their plans.

During the 1860s as many as eighty ships arrived in Victoria from San Francisco each month.[8] The St. Nicholas Hotel guest list, published weekly in the newspaper, included doctors, lawyers, sea captains, and comparable members of the wealthy classes. Most of the hotel's clientele arrived from the United States, but some guests who booked into the St. Nicholas came from as far away as Germany.

Mr. and Mrs. J. Fried owned and managed the St. Nicholas Hotel from 1867 to 1872. During this time all of the rooms were refurnished in the most up-to-date fashion, an expensive undertaking to be sure. "One half of the building [was] divided off for purposes of a restaurant"—doubling the restaurant in size—"while the hall and the majority of the rooms [were] maintained by Mr. Fried."[9] The new catchword for the first-class hotel was "cleanliness and good order." In addition, Fried introduced apartment suites that rented by the day, week, and month. Fried also added a skating rink inside the St. Nicholas Hall, which was a big hit with the public.[10]

In December 1872 the hotel was leased to J.L. Frankland with the understanding that the St. Nicholas would continue to operate as a first-class hotel. By June 1873 Charles H. Trevitt, an experienced hotelier from the United States, was leasing the St. Nicholas Hotel. This lasted for a brief time, until partners Charles Trehart and E.F. Hemenover took over the lease; they held it from 1873 to 1879. In June 1879 Trehart was granted a transfer of the liquor licence to the old Boomerang Inn on Langley Street, where he set up his business; his partner, Hemenover, had left some six months earlier.[11] The owner, the now-widowed Mrs. Fried, operated the St Nicholas Hotel for the next few years.

In 1881 Bernard F. Dillion purchased the fifty-room St. Nicholas Hotel. Dillion came from County Longford, Ireland. Over the years, each new proprietor had made improvements to the hotel that helped maintain its first-class status. Dillion continued the trend by adding a new floor with ten more rooms and reopening the bar, with John Welsh as head bartender. Dillion retained a number of the apartments, which continued to be rented out on a weekly or monthly basis. After selling the hotel to John McCartney in 1885, Dillion purchased a small saloon in Esquimalt and then moved to Portland, Oregon, where he died at the age of forty-five.

The Oriental Hotel, 550 Yates Street, in 1884, proudly showing off their new addition.

McCartney operated the St. Nicholas Hotel until 1888, when his application to transfer his licence to the Snug Tavern on Douglas Street was refused. McCartney sold the hotel to Charles Pagden, who immediately changed the name from the St. Nicholas to the Delmonico Hotel. McCartney could not get a licence approved for the Snug Tavern; he tore it down and replaced it with the Leland House in September 1889, which was granted a licence. He sold that hotel in 1891 and moved to the Cariboo, where he had some success in mining. He died from heart disease in December 1893.[12]

The Delmonico Hotel continued the tradition of providing first-class service to its customers until August 1899, when its name was changed to the Savoy Hotel.

ORIENTAL HOTEL
1862–1908

Pietro Manetta opened the Oriental Hotel as a two-storey wood building on the northeast corner of (46) 550 Yates Street and Oriental Alley in 1862. The hotel offered two bars, a billiards saloon, and rooms where guests could sleep in comfort on new beds featuring spring mattresses. Manetta was a prolific hotelman. He had recently sold the Miner's Exchange Saloon (which he owned from 1858 to 1861) and had leased the saloon in the Bayley's Hotel in 1859. He now owned the Oriental Hotel, which he would operate until 1867 before moving on to the Blue Post Saloon.

The fact that the Oriental Hotel had two bars, one off Yates Street and the other on Oriental Alley, caught the eye of the licensing board. In April 1862 the bartender of the Oriental Hotel was arrested for selling liquor without a licence. Manetta fought the arrest in court, stating that he was the sole owner of both bars within his establishment and that his single liquor licence should be sufficient to cover both. The judge agreed with him, thereby setting a precedent "that a man may sell liquor from as many bars as he likes, provided they are all under one roof and the proceeds are realized by the person in whose name the license is obtained."[13]

J. Jeffree, the proprietor of the Union Saloon, and Manetta had a very public dispute that played out in the *Colonist*.[14] Jeffree was one of Manetta's employees at the Miner's Exchange Saloon on Johnson Street until he quit and opened a saloon next door. The two businesses were in fierce competition, which added to their mutual disdain. Jeffree accused Manetta of using his liquor licence from the Oriental Hotel for the Miner's Exchange Saloon, which Manetta denied in a letter to the editor. It was learned that Manetta had three liquor licences, one for each of his saloons in town and a country licence for his hotel in Sooke, and therefore had not violated the law.

In 1868 Manetta sold the Oriental Hotel to William McKeon and Charles H. Trehart. McKeon operated the hotel from 1868 to 1905—a total of thirty-seven years, the longest tenure of any owner. These years saw many changes as the Oriental Hotel was twice expanded and business boomed. McKeon bought out Trehart in December 1873 to become the sole owner.

In September 1876 an advertisement appeared in the local

ORIENTAL HOTEL.

Wm. McKeon, Proprietor, Yates st., Victoria, B.C.
Centrally located. Rooms single or in suits. No
dark rooms. Meals at all hours. Charges moderate.
Private Dining Rooms for ladies.

Advertisement for the Oriental Hotel, *British Colonist*, April 1884.

newspaper calling for tenders for a planned three-storey brick building beside the Oriental Hotel on Yates Street. The building would be erected east of the original wood structure and designed by well-known architect John Teague, who used the new and exciting iron technology. Precast structural components from San Francisco foundries allowed for facades to be opened up far beyond the limits of brick technology, resulting in spectacularly innovative architecture not yet seen in Victoria.[15]

In April 1883 work began on the new Oriental Hotel. It opened on January 9, 1884, at the cost of $14,000. The new three-storey brick addition was far more attractive than the two-storey wood-framed original, now outdated and worn. The magnificent addition was in the Victorian Italianate style, with cast-iron columns supporting the splendid detailing of the facade, complete with tall, ornate bay windows and ground-floor arches. The renovated hotel became an instant hit with the travelling public and aided in its transformation to a truly first-class establishment. Travellers desired a well-lit room, and the bay windows offered an excellent view of the city and the activities on Yates Street.

The new thirty-six-room Oriental Hotel was advertised as "a first-class family hotel, no dark rooms, table served with all the delicacies of the season. This hotel has just been built and everything is new and perfect."[16]

The Oriental Hotel was expanded again in 1888 when the last part of the original wood building was removed and replaced with the same style of brick as the 1883 addition by builders Smith and Clark. The attention to detail in both the exterior and interior reflected the fashion of the day and resulted in the most modern hotel of its time.

In 1907 G.W. Weeks and A.J. Rolph purchased the hotel. The following year they changed the name to the St. Francis. The St. Francis Hotel lasted long after Prohibition, closing in 1956. It sat vacant until 1958, when it reopened as a Salvation Army Thrift Store. The historic building still stands today and was recently renovated into condominiums.

DRIARD HOTEL
1872–1910

The Driard Hotel was the best-known and most luxurious hotel in North America in the 1890s, equal in importance to Victoria as Claridge's to London or the Waldorf Astoria to New York.[17] The hotel began as the St. George in 1861 under the ownership of Madame L.A. Bendixen, who ran it until her death in 1866. Bendixen was born in France and made her way to Victoria through San Francisco. She hired architects Saunders and

Sosthenes Driard, proprietor of the Colonial, St. George, and Driard Hotels.
IMAGE #A-02117 COURTESY OF THE ROYAL BC MUSEUM AND ARCHIVES

Wright, who designed the attractive four-storey brick structure complete with a mansard roof and a single cupola as the crown on top.[18] A flag raised on a pole attached to the cupola signalled the arrival of the steamer carrying mail from San Francisco.

The St. George had two short-term proprietors from 1866 until August 1871, when Sosthenes Maximilian Driard purchased the hotel for the bargain price of $5,500, a fraction of what it and

The Driard Hotel, most prestigious in Victoria until the Empress Hotel opened in 1908.

the land on which it sat were worth. Driard used the St. George as an annex to his Colonial Hotel. In May 1872 he changed the name to the Driard House and immediately went to work renovating the hotel by adding thirty-four rooms, each with its own fireplace, for a total of one hundred rooms.[19]

Sosthenes Driard was born in Chapelle-la-Reine, France, in 1819. He came to Victoria from San Francisco in 1858 and soon purchased the modest Colonial Hotel on Government Street. Driard managed the restaurant while his partner, Prosper Grelley, ran the hotel. Driard and Grelley built up the business, reinvesting and continually improving their hotel. Driard then bought out his partner in 1861, making him the sole owner of the Colonial Hotel until his death in February 1873. Having received his training as a chef in Paris, Driard gained an excellent reputation for his culinary skills at the Colonial Restaurant and later at the Driard House.[20]

In February 1873 Driard fell ill with apoplexy and died four days later at the age of fifty-four.[21] Two years later his precious Colonial Hotel, a business Driard had nurtured for fourteen years, was destroyed by fire.[22] Under the new management of Louis Redon and A. Lucas, the Driard House continued the tradition begun by Sosthenes Driard of providing excellent food and service to its patrons.

On October 1, 1882, the upper floors of the Driard House were damaged by a fire that started across the street at Bowman's Stables. The *Colonist* reported that the entire upper level of the Driard House, including the decorative cupola, was destroyed. The loss to the owners of the Driard was estimated at $25,000, but they were insured for only $8,000.[23] There came a silver lining from the disastrous fire, however, as Redon and Lucas rebuilt their hotel bigger and better than before. "Thanks to the design of architect John Teague, a completely new Driard House emerged from the ashes, grander and more elegant than what had gone on before." [24]

From 1883 to 1892 the Driard Hotel went through a series of expansions and upgrades. The upper floors were repaired and expanded over the Victoria Theatre, which had opened in 1885 at View and Douglas Streets, and a grander hotel entrance was built off Douglas Street. [25] One hundred rooms were added, for a total of 225 rooms. The new Driard Hotel, opened on November 1, 1892, by Ernest Escalet, was in a class by itself. The famous artist and writer Emily Carr noted, "Victoria's top grandness was the Driard Hotel; all important visitors stayed at the Driard. The Driard was a brick building with big doors that swung and squeaked. It was red inside and out. It had soft red carpets, sofas and chairs upholstered in red plush and red curtains." [26]

The timing of the Driard's reopening couldn't have been better. Vancouver had surpassed Victoria in population and importance, but tourism helped fill the vacuum of revenue lost from businesses moving to the mainland. In the previous ten years there had been a serious shortage of hotel rooms in the city, and the Driard helped fill the gap. [27] The new six-storey Driard Hotel cost $275,000, of which $30,000 went to plumbing.

The magnificent mahogany-filled bar was managed by Robert J. Campbell, who had worked the previous six years in the Drum Saloon, which was located in one of the most luxurious hotels in Seattle. Campbell spent $6,000 on the bar, with the local Sehl, Hastie, Erskine Furniture Company providing most of the fixtures. He also hired "the ablest mixers of the day." [28] Having the Victoria Theatre within the Driard Hotel complex meant that theatre-goers could "slip into the red leather and brass bar for a quick drink between acts." [29]

There were few hotels that could compete with the magnificent Driard Hotel; the Mount Baker Hotel in Oak Bay was one of them. Unfortunately, the Mount Baker was completely destroyed by fire in 1902, and its replacement was much smaller and less elaborate. It wasn't until 1908 when the Driard Hotel was finally surpassed in splendour by the Empress Hotel.

Since 1901 there had been talk of the Canadian Pacific Railway either purchasing an existing hotel or building a brand new tourist hotel in Victoria. At one time the Driard and Western Hotels were considered, but decisions were delayed. Suffice to say the Canadian Pacific president, Sir Thomas Shaughnessy, checked into the Driard Hotel in August 1902 to attend a meeting to discuss building the Empress Hotel.

The Empress opened on January 20, 1908. The details regarding the building of the hotel are shared later in this chapter, but during the four years it took to build, most hotel owners feared that their business would be affected by the opening of such a prestigious and large hotel. However, "the worst fears of local hotel owners were not realized. Within two years of the Empress opening, the Driard would be renovated and freshened from cellar to attic." [30]

By 1910 the new owners of the Driard, Sol Cameron and Parker Clarke, were pleased with the recent renovations that had updated the hotel. They had every reason to be optimistic about the future, but then came the Five Sisters fire. On October 26, 1910, a fire broke out in Spencer's Department Store located across Broad Street near the Driard Hotel. Strong winds fanned the flames, allowing the fire to quickly gain momentum and get out of control. By the time it was extinguished the fire had destroyed most of the buildings within the Five Sisters Block bounded by Government, Fort, Broad, and Trounce Streets, but the Driard sustained only some fire and water damage. "Driard's narrow escape," began one newspaper account at the time. "During the fiercest part of the fire, the intense heat licked off the metal cornices on the Driard Hotel igniting the woodwork on the gables and window sills, but streams of water from the fire hoses as well as from within saved the building. The greatest damage to the hotel premises will be from water." [31]

This was the last straw for the hotel's owners; with their money tied up in costly renovations, expensive repairs due to the fire were just too much to face. When David Spencer lost his department store business and offered to buy the damaged Driard Hotel, the owners jumped at the chance, and so ended the greatest luxury hotel of its time.

DOMINION HOTEL
1876–2005

There has been a hotel on the southwest corner of Yates and Blanshard Streets since the What Cheer House opened in 1858 (see Chapter One), but there are no references to the What Cheer House after 1866. The first mention of the Dominion House was

Dominion Hotel, Victoria, B.C.

The Dominion Hotel, 759 Yates Street.

when the *Colonist* reported that a meeting had taken place there on May 25, 1870, but the Dominion House, later renamed the Dominion Hotel, may have opened as early as 1867. We do know that Thomas Smith opened a Dominion House on Government Street in 1871, and five years later Mrs. Gerow owned the Dominion House at (117) 759 Yates Street.

Stephen Jones purchased the two-storey wood structure from Mrs. Gerow in December 1876 for $2,500.[32] It was the beginning of a hotel dynasty in which three generations of the Jones family built the small hostelry from an obscure boarding house into one of the premier hotels of Victoria.

Jones was born in Milltown, County Kerry, Ireland, in 1817. He immigrated to Canada and lived in Clinton, Ontario, until moving to Victoria in 1872.[33] Jones was experienced in the hospitality industry, successfully running the Orleans Hotel on Cormorant Street since 1874. Five months after purchasing the Dominion House, Jones put it up for sale, but by September 1877, with no takers, Jones decided to retain and refurbish the Dominion House and offer weekly room and board for six dollars.

Jones kept himself busy, not only improving the Dominion House but also purchasing the International Hotel in Esquimalt in 1881, which he operated until 1885. In December 1888 Jones was refused the renewal of his liquor licence for the Dominion Hotel due to fear of fire in the old wooden building. In March 1889 Jones decided it was time to retire and turn the business over to his eldest son and namesake, Stephen, who was just twenty years old.

Stephen Jones Jr. attempted to license his bar at the old

Dominion Hotel in March 1898, but like his father, he was refused a licence due to the potential fire hazard. Jones planned to demolish the old building and replace it with a larger modern brick building. "The old Dominion Hotel on Yates Street is doomed. It has been an old landmark and has witnessed Victoria's progress since way back in the '50s, but now it has to give way to the onward march of improvement. It will be demolished to make room for a more modern and commodious structure. The new building will have a frontage of 55 feet and a depth of 52 feet with three storeys and a basement."[34] This was the first of many reincarnations through renovations for the Dominion Hotel over the years.

Under the direction of contractors Elford and Smith, the handsome three-storey, late–Victorian Italianate Dominion Hotel began to take shape on Yates Street just west of the original wood building. When it was completed it won great praise from the travelling public and joined the ranks of the more prestigious hotels of Victoria. The elder Jones had lived to see the opening of the wonderful new hotel. He enjoyed a very productive life in the hotel business, having owned four successful hotels over the years. He died at 10 AM on Monday, November 20, 1893, from bronchitis. Mrs. Jones and their family of nine, their friends, and the public packed into the Dominion Hotel to pay their respects to a true pioneer.

The Dominion Hotel continued to prosper under the capable hands of Stephen Jones Jr. In 1898 architect Samuel Maclure designed an addition to the hotel, expanding it 33 feet to the east on Yates Street toward Blanshard Street and 120 feet deep. The addition would give the hotel a total of 106 well-lit

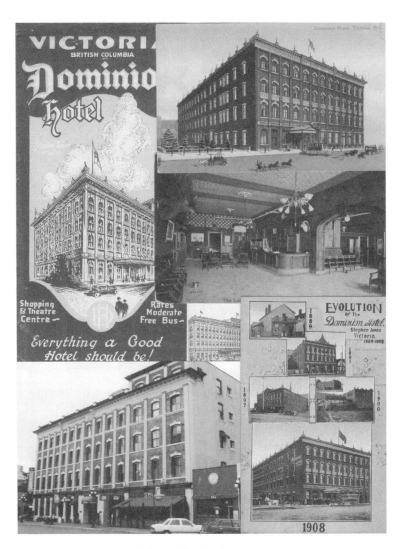

Collage of the Dominion Hotel.
GLEN A. MOFFORD POSTCARD COLLECTION AND PHOTOGRAPHS

rooms, half of them with baths. The older section of the hotel was refitted with steam heat and electric lights to match the addition. The exterior facade matched the original 1891 building. When the $20,000 renovation was finished, an advertisement in the *Colonist* in January 1898, complete with illustration, boasted that the Dominion Hotel was now the largest hotel west of Toronto.[35] A free coach was used to pick up and drop off guests at their convenience.

On September 28, 1898, various hotel owners were asked what they believed would happen if prohibition closed down their respective hotel bars. Stephen Jones Jr. reflected many of the owners' feelings when he claimed that it would be "impossible to conduct a hotel successfully without a bar. Temperance hotels were inferior and a failure everywhere. Victoria had perhaps for its size the best popular priced hotels in Canada, but they could not be run without bars."[36] Indeed, the Dominion Hotel had a splendid bar, operated by bartender Harry Maloney since 1891, that brought in a significant portion of the hotel's revenue. Unlike the old hostelry, the new Dominion Hotel no longer had a problem obtaining and renewing its liquor licence.

In 1907 the last of the major additions to the Dominion Hotel took place. A fourth floor, designed by Thomas Hooper, was added to the hotel. The grand Dominion Hotel now loomed large over Yates Street and joined the unique group of first-class hotels in the city. The Dominion Hotel consistently served the public from 1876, when Stephen Jones bought a small boarding house on Yates Street, up to 2005, when an American hotel chain bought the establishment and changed its name to the Dalton Hotel.

CLARENCE HOTEL
1886–1922

The Clarence Hotel opened in September 1886 on the northeast corner of 1303–1307 Douglas and (102) 702 Yates Streets, with Frank G. Richards Jr. as proprietor. The spacious and handsome four-storey brick and stone Clarence Hotel was designed by J.P. Donovan and built by J. Coughlan.

The new hotel was the talk of the town when it officially opened on September 4, 1886. The first floor contained an excellent bar that measured twenty-five feet by forty feet. It was elaborately crafted in Spanish cedar, maple, ash, and mahogany, with luxurious bar fixtures manufactured by Brunswick & Balke of Chicago. A billiard table and pool table could be found inside the bar. A reading room and the hotel office were next to the bar, and the grand entrance from Douglas Street opened onto the lobby, with its sweeping main staircase to the second floor. The second floor, which could also be accessed by elevator, contained a three-hundred-seat, twenty-six-by-forty-foot public dining room; a private dining room and parlour exclusively for guests of the hotel; a large kitchen with a range manufactured by Albion Iron Works of Victoria; and nine suites. The furnishings in the second-floor rooms were mostly of ash or walnut with marble tops manufactured in London, Ontario. The third floor contained the ladies' parlour, three suites, and eighteen rooms, and the top floor had twenty-six rooms, each with an electric bell, and two bathrooms on either end of the hall.[37] Also incorporated into the hotel building, and certainly handy for guests of the Clarence,

The Clarence Hotel on the northeast corner of Douglas and Yates Streets.
IMAGE #E-01551 COURTESY OF THE ROYAL BC MUSEUM AND ARCHIVES

was a second-floor bowling alley and shooting gallery above Yates Street managed by James Baker.[38]

Clubs and societies were eager to book their events at the newest luxury hotel in Victoria. The BC Pioneer Society held its annual dinner and dance there, as did the St. George's Society. The Victoria Lodge of the Independent Order of Odd Fellows (IOOF) celebrated its twenty-fifth anniversary at the Clarence Hotel, and countless other clubs kept the hotel busy with bookings.

Richards may have learned a thing or two about the hospitality industry from his father, Frank G. Richards Sr., who ran Uncle Frank's Saloon on Langley Street. Having made a wise investment in a successful copper mine in Sooke, Richards Jr. sold the lease of the Clarence Hotel to W.C. Anderson in October 1888 and went on to make a fortune in real estate. In 1902 Richards successfully ran for sheriff.

Anderson left his position as steward of the Union Club to become the proprietor of the popular Clarence Hotel. Tragedy struck the Anderson family, however, when son John ended his own life. John Anderson had become smitten with a pretty, young blond woman in "a disreputable house" on Broughton Street. Apparently she went by various names and aliases, including Annie Johnson and Ella Marston. The younger Anderson's infatuation with the prostitute found him following her to Seattle, where, in the Two Johns Saloon, he attempted to talk to her. She ignored his advances, so the impulsive and depressed Anderson went back to his hotel room and shot himself in his right side. The doctor could not save him and he died twelve hours later.[39]

No major incidents took place in the Clarence Hotel in its early years other than a few thefts. A man named Charlie was arrested for stealing articles from the rooms and was reported as "in limbo" at the local jail.[40] On another occasion a few customers complained that the boots they had put out in the hall to be polished had gone missing. On further investigation it was learned that the thief most likely wore a size 6.

From 1889 to 1898 the Clarence Hotel went through five proprietors. Business at the first-class hotel remained steady year-round as the hotel advertised lower winter rates to attract borders in the colder months. The hotel was also a favourite place for sealing captains who would stay there in the off-season. The Klondike Gold Rush gave every hotel and business in town a helping hand as prospectors would return to Victoria in the wet, cold winter months to let loose in the hotel bars and saloons while spending their poke (gold dust) round town.

Mr. and Mrs. A.R. McDonald became the new proprietors of the Clarence Hotel in January 1898. They immediately changed its name to the Australian Hotel (by this time the original Australian House was called the Bay View Hotel).[41] Shortly after they took over as proprietors, a serious incident occurred in the hotel. Parker McKenzie, a guest travelling to the Klondike from the Puget Sound area, accidentally left the gas jet open after extinguishing the flame of his lamp. The next morning McDonald was walking down the hall when he smelled the gas; he found the room it was coming from and had to get the extra key to enter, as there was no answer to his knock. He found McKenzie dead in his bed.[42] It was confirmed at a subsequent inquest that the man had died from asphyxiation.

The Dallas Hotel, Dallas Road in James Bay, 1891.
GLEN A. MOFFORD POSTCARD COLLECTION AND PHOTOGRAPHS

In January 1899 McDonald changed the name of the Australian Hotel back to its best-known name, the Clarence Hotel. He then sold the lease to James Adam and John Skinner, who operated it for less than six months before they sold the lease to Henry Harris. Harris would operate the hotel for the next eleven years, until 1911.

After October 1917 and Prohibition, the Clarence Hotel bar initially managed to remain open by selling an inferior product called "near beer" and offering patrons free lunches and billiards. But it was just a matter of time before the bar would close its doors. The Clarence Hotel stayed in business until 1922, when the owners sold it to the Bank of Nova Scotia and the once magnificent Clarence Hotel building was demolished.

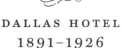

DALLAS HOTEL
1891–1926

The Dallas Hotel opened on Dallas Road and Simcoe Street in 1891. The hotel was named for Alexander Grant Dallas, the son-in-law of Sir James Douglas, and was designed by Edward McCoskrie. McCoskrie was also commissioned by William Jensen, the first proprietor of the Dallas Hotel, to design six houses on Superior Street and three stores on Dallas Road.[43]

The handsome three-storey hotel contained sixty luxury rooms, many with bay windows that offered a commanding view of the Strait of Juan de Fuca and the Olympic Mountains. The hotel also had a distinctive central tower topped by a flagpole.

The hotel advertised itself as "The Only Seaside Hotel in Victoria, BC," and it stood out as a magnificent addition along the James Bay waterfront. Jensen purposely chose the waterfront location close to Ogden Point Docks and nearby Rithet's Outer Wharves where the ocean steamers berthed. Passengers were met by the Dallas Hotel carriage for a short and pleasant ride to the hotel.[44]

Born in Liverpool, England, in 1840 to Danish parents, William Jensen immigrated to the United States in 1858. He joined the army fighting for the Federal side in the American Civil War. After the war he worked in private business in New York until 1868. Jensen then moved to Kansas, where he built his first hotel. In 1872 he moved to California, then made his way north to Seattle, where he ran the American Exchange Saloon until he left for Victoria in 1877.[45] As a man of means, Jensen could afford to spend money. Upon arriving in Victoria he purchased the Occidental Hotel on the corner of Johnson and Wharf Streets. He then purchased the old Royal Hotel on Wharf Street next to the Occidental, which was then an import and export business, and absorbed it into his expanding hotel. Jensen was the proprietor of the Occidental Hotel from 1877 to 1883. He leased out the hotel for a time, but came back to run it from 1889 to 1891, when he built the Dallas Hotel.

When it opened, the Dallas Hotel was praised as a first-class establishment. The hotel could accommodate up to one hundred guests and offered the most modern conveniences, such as steam-heated rooms, hot and cold running water, electric lights, and electric call bells in each room for prompt service. The Dallas Hotel offered patrons a special feature: a 125-by-65-foot

The Dallas Hotel after renovations added a new roof.

viewing room on the flat roof of the hotel, in which delighted guests could marvel at the 360-degree view high above the street.

At street level, the spacious hotel bar offered a waterfront view and a separate billiards and games room. Jensen was granted a liquor licence on July 29, 1891. Less than five months later Jensen found himself in hot water. The new Sunday blue law prohibited the sale of alcoholic beverages on the Sabbath to the general public, though registered guests could imbibe. The law took effect on Friday, January 1, 1892, and Jensen was the first to be charged in violation of the act when on Sunday, January 3, he allowed a non-registered customer a beer. He was found guilty and was ordered to pay court costs and a twenty-dollar fine.[46]

The significance of the Jensen case was that liquor regulations were tightening. Gone were the days of the wide-open saloon as more restrictions were applied to bar and saloon owners and liquor licences became more difficult to obtain. These changes began in the mid-1880s, and as we will see in Chapter Five, "Restriction to Prohibition," they altered the saloon and hotel industry forever.

In September 1898 Jensen was asked what effect prohibition might have on his business. He replied that without a bar, a first-class hotel like the Dallas could not operate. Prohibition would prove detrimental to the city as a whole, and to non-temperance hotels in particular, and property values would plummet as a result of a glut of unproductive real estate on the market. The existing licensing system was appropriate and acted as a deterrent against crimes such as bootlegging.[47]

In 1900 William Jensen sold the Dallas Hotel to Mrs. Marion N. Walt, but continued his long and distinguished career in the hotel industry as the new proprietor of the Dawson Hotel at

641 Yates Street. The Dawson became the King Edward Hotel in 1904 (profiled in this chapter). But Jensen didn't stop there. After he left the Dawson Hotel in 1903 he purchased the Sidney Hotel, considered a first-class resort, and ran it until 1909. Jensen died in 1914 at the age of seventy-four and was buried in Ross Bay Cemetery.

Proprietress Walt also kept the Vernon Hotel at the corner of Douglas and View Streets, which she purchased in 1900 and ran until 1906, as well as the first-class Victoria Hotel, which she purchased sometime between 1899 and 1901. Mrs. Walt started the tradition of holding weekly concerts performed by the 5th Regiment band in the spacious ballroom at the Dallas. These concerts were very popular and attracted large crowds.[48] The Dallas also hosted the dinners and dances of numerous clubs and societies, such as the Lawn Tennis Club, which saw 150 couples and a number of officers from the Esquimalt naval station participate in their dance at the hotel. "Mrs. Walt had been indefatigable in her efforts to make the affair a brilliant success, and she succeeded admirably. The ball room decorations were of a most elaborate and beautiful character and the floor in perfect condition."[49]

On December 24, 1901, work began on extensive alterations and additions at the Dallas Hotel. A fourth storey and new roof were added, giving the hotel a brand new appearance. The contract was awarded to Thomas Catterall and was completed in record time. The remodelled Dallas reopened on February 15, 1902. The proprietorship also changed when Marion Walt's new husband, James Patterson, joined her as an owner of the hotel in 1903. On December 20, 1905, the Pattersons sold the hotel to James's parents, Isabella and William Patterson.

A familiar theme was played out in December 1907 when William and Isabella Patterson were charged with selling liquor on a Sunday. It came out in court that a William Lang had collapsed while having lunch at the Dallas Hotel and glasses of brandy and port wine were fetched to restore him. A short time later it was revealed that Lang was drunk, not from being served from the bar or restaurant, but from a bottle that he had kept in his room.[50]

On August 7, 1908, William died from heart failure, leaving his widow, Isabella, as the sole proprietor of the Dallas Hotel. Isabella operated the hotel successfully until her death in 1912. Perry Criddle was the proprietor of the Dallas Hotel from 1912 to 1918, the last proprietor prior to Prohibition. Herbert McCall was the head bartender at the Dallas until he lost his job when the bar closed in October 1917.

The Dallas Hotel saw a succession of managers come and go between 1918 and 1922. Arthur Evans was the last to manage the fading hotel, from 1922 to 1926. By this time the grand hotel was showing her age, and without the revenue from the bar, the proprietor could no longer afford the renovations and upkeep required for such a large establishment. Just as William Jensen had predicted in 1898, without the important revenue from selling spirits and beer from the bar, the hotel could not continue to attract customers. But there were other reasons for the demise of the Dallas beyond lost revenue due to Prohibition. The Dallas Hotel was simply out of date, a white elephant. The dredging of the inner harbour allowed passenger ships to steam right past the Dallas and dock directly in front of the Empress and within a short distance from downtown hotels.

Evans managed to stay in business until 1926, when he reluctantly closed the doors for good. The combination of high taxes, reduced revenue, and high maintenance costs all contributed to the end of the Dallas Hotel. It sat vacant and boarded up for two years until it was demolished in 1928.

VICTORIA HOTEL (III)
1892–1917

The eighty-four-suite Victoria Hotel was opened on March 13, 1892, on the northwest corner of (140) 1400–1406 Government Street and Johnson Street by P.T. Patton. This was the third hotel to have that name, and it was by far the most luxurious. The first Victoria Hotel, situated on the corner of Courtney and Government Streets, had been renamed the Windsor Hotel, and the second Victoria Hotel, located on the corner of Fort and Douglas Streets, lasted only from 1889 to January 1897.

Born in Montreal, P.T. Patton grew up in the hotel business. His father was proprietor of the St. Lawrence Hall Hotel. In 1879 Patton travelled to Denver, where he worked in the hotel business until 1891, when he moved to Victoria.[51] Patton worked as a fruit vendor on Yates Street for a brief time, until he opened the Victoria Hotel a year later.

The Victoria Hotel received glowing praise in the *Colonist* after a reporter was given a thirty-minute tour of the new hotel. He described it as one of the finest first-class hotels in the country. "From top to bottom the place is furnished utterly regardless

The Victoria Hotel (III), northwest corner of Johnson and Government Streets.

of expense . . . the ceilings and walls have been frescoed very artistically with various views, while the hall ceiling is painted with large clusters of yellow roses. One of the doors takes the visitor into the large barroom which is garnished with mahogany and black walnut, and like the office, is also frescoed elaborately. Next to the bar is the short-order restaurant [with] the entrance off Government Street."[52] Generous use of solid carved oak and mahogany could be found throughout the Victoria Hotel.

In a short-lived partnership, architects Thomas Hooper and Samuel May Goddard designed the extensive and elaborate Wilson-Dalby Block, which ran from the corner of Johnson Street north along the west side of 1400–1480 Government Street. The three-storey brick Victoria Hotel occupied the corner to 1406 Government Street.[53] The hotel was located on one of the busiest intersections of the commercial downtown core, within easy distance to trains and the docks. Everything about the Victoria Hotel was first-class, from the furnishings supplied by the Sehl, Hastie, Erskine Furniture Company to the fine menu. The chef, M. Benard, had spent the previous eight years in the kitchens of the renowned Palace Hotel in San Francisco. F.J. Cotta, the head steward, directed his staff professionally to ensure that guests were satisfied.[54]

The Victoria Hotel was granted a liquor licence on March 20, 1892. During the Christmas season, patrons in the bar were invited to enjoy free eggnog and a scrumptious lunch. A tournament of English billiards was held in the games room off the bar in which eighteen players vied for prizes put up by Patton, and concerts and dances were held in the grand ballroom, where the refreshments flowed along with the music.

Patton did not stay long at his new hotel, retiring to his home at Firwood Lodge in Victoria. He sold the hotel to Ernest Escalet in October 1894. Escalet continued the first-class service begun by Patton through the difficult economic downturn in the mid-1890s. In 1896 Escalet decided to explore a business opportunity in Nelson, BC, and sold the Victoria Hotel to A.R. McDonald. McDonald was the proprietor for a mere four months before he, too, sold. Between 1896 and 1901 the Victoria Hotel had five different proprietors.

One notable proprietor certainly worth mentioning was Captain John Claus Voss, who ran the Victoria Hotel from 1897 to 1899. Captain Voss was a hotelier, an adventurer, and a well-known man about town. His claim to fame would come in 1900 when he sailed a thirty-eight-foot canoe around the world.[55] The Tilikum dugout canoe was made from an ancient red cedar tree purchased from the Siwash Band.[56] Captain Voss also owned the Queens Hotel from 1896 to 1900 and purchased the Oriental Hotel on Yates Street when he returned from his long voyage around the globe in 1904. There was also a rumour that Captain Voss had smuggled Chinese migrant workers into British Columbia and kept them hidden in the basement of the Queens Hotel on Johnson Street.[57]

The economic downturn of the mid-1890s was quickly replaced by the salad days of 1898 brought on by the Klondike Gold Rush. The very competent but hard-nosed Captain Voss maintained a first-class hotel. In October 1898 he had a falling-out with the manager of the hotel, W.H. Maudsley, who sued Voss for wrongful dismissal.[58] At some point between 1899 and 1901, Voss sold the Victoria Hotel to Mrs. Marion N. Walt, who also owned the Vernon and Dallas Hotels at the time.

From 1900 to 1917 there were ten different proprietors of the

Victoria Hotel. By 1914 the hotel was in a slow decline. Weekly room rates dropped from three to two dollars. In September 1915 William Taylor, manager of the Victoria Hotel, was arrested and charged with keeping "a disorderly house," while two young ladies were charged with "being the inmates of that house."[59]

Joseph Balagno was the final proprietor of the Victoria Hotel before Prohibition closed the bar and deprived the business of much-needed revenue, which further hastened the demise of the grand old hotel. Like the Dallas and Driard Hotels before it, the Victoria Hotel became less important and could no longer compete with the renewed Dominion and King Edward Hotels or, especially, the magnificent Empress Hotel.

KING EDWARD HOTEL
1904–17

The King Edward was the smallest of the first-class hotels but by no means was it any less luxurious or spectacular. The two-storey brick building dated back to 1891 when it opened as the New York Hotel. It became the Dawson Hotel during the Klondike Gold Rush of 1898 and kept that name until 1903, when it was changed to the St. Charles Hotel. Under new proprietors Marion and James Patterson, the St. Charles became the King Edward Hotel in honour of King Edward VII. Like the Victoria Hotel, the King Edward was located in the heart of the commercial core in downtown Victoria at (65–69) 641 Yates Street between Broad and Douglas Streets.

The rotunda at the King Edward Hotel.
GLEN A. MOFFORD COLLECTION

The Pattersons were also the proprietors of the Dallas Hotel, and Marion was the sole proprietor of the Vernon Hotel during this time. The Pattersons set about renovating the King Edward before the ink was dry on their purchase contract. The old hotel was updated throughout and expanded. They also bought the adjoining Orpheum Theatre, which had been closed for some time, and turned it into a first-class dining room.[60]

As with most first-class hotels, the guests checking into the King Edward were people of means: doctors, lawyers, politicians (like A.E. Planta, the mayor of Nanaimo), and people of industry. The hotel was also a popular destination for newly married couples to spend their honeymoon, as stated in the following announcement: "Mr. and Mrs. B. Lindsay of Vancouver, were in Victoria during the past week spending their honeymoon. They occupied the bridal chamber of the King Edward Hotel making twenty-two newly married couples who have occupied this room since the opening of the hotel in February last."[61]

On Christmas Day, 1905, the proprietor, Marion Patterson, was presented with a "fine electric sign" by Mr. R. Wilson of the Canadian Pacific Railway. It was later attached above the main entrance to the King Edward Hotel on Yates Street, which made for an attractive addition to the hotel. The gift came with good wishes of the season from the regular boarders and a number of the commercial travellers who made the King Edward their home away from home.[62]

A substantial alteration was made to the King Edward Hotel in December 1906. The BC Hardware Company occupied the ground floor next to the King Edward on the corner of Yates and Broad Streets. While the BC Hardware Company building was being renovated and updated, a third floor was added to match the three storeys of the King Edward (the Pattersons had added a third), and the hotel then occupied the two floors above the hardware store. The contract was given to Thomas Catterall & Sons, and the work cost $20,000. Fifty new suites were added, each with a self-contained bathroom, electric lights, and "telephone communications."[63] The plumbing was state of the art, a system known as the "Durham system," which had also recently been installed in the yet-to-open Canadian Pacific Railway hotel on Government Street.

In 1908 Mr. and Mrs. Charles Alfred Hamilton purchased the King Edward Hotel and continued to improve and expand the business, paying $300 for a small brick addition. The Hamiltons hired William (Billy) McAllister as head bartender. McAllister moved to the Alberni Valley in 1912 to run the New Alberni Hotel until 1918.

The same year that the Hamiltons bought the King Edward Hotel, the Empress Hotel opened. The brand new Empress Hotel, owned by the Canadian Pacific Railway, was the talk of the town. The travelling public and locals alike fell in love with this marvellous new hostelry, while local hotel owners feared that the new hotel would take away their business. But the hotel owners soon learned that their fears were unfounded as there were enough customers to go around and fill all of the hotels. Indeed, if there was a problem, it was that there were not enough rooms for the number of visitors to Victoria over the following few years. Curiosity and excitement over the opening of the Empress resulted in a full house from which customers had to be turned away. The other hotels began to see a sharp rise in their business. Over the next three years all of the first-class hotels, such as the Empress, the Driard, the Dominion, the Victoria, and the King Edward, were filled to capacity and in many cases had to turn travellers away. "The King Edward has been full these past five weeks," read one newspaper account in 1910.[64]

The hotels were benefitting from the economic boom that preceded the First World War, which was to begin in August 1914. From 1910 to 1913 a building frenzy occurred that kept contractors very busy with new projects. The tourist industry was also at its zenith as more travellers arrived in Victoria than ever before. The King Edward Hotel was a well-known destination hotel that enjoyed a good reputation. By 1912 the King Edward had a total of ninety-eight bedrooms—forty-eight with attached baths—a seventy-eight-seat dining room, a popular bar with a billiards room, and new proprietors, F.L. Wolfenden and W.A. Millington.

The new proprietors set about updating the furnishings in

The lobby of the King Edward Hotel.
GLEN A. MOFFORD POSTCARD COLLECTION

Empress Hotel, Victoria, B. C.

The Empress Hotel in 1907, a few months before opening.

all of the rooms. They hired Maynard & Sons Auctioneers to sell outdated items, which included iron bedsteads, springs, felt mattresses, solid oak dressers, chairs, couches, and tables. All were in excellent condition. Everything, right down to the bed sheets, was sold at auction and replaced with the brand new and modern.

An unfortunate incident took place in the back of the bar at the King Edward Hotel during this period. A number of soldiers had been drinking and laughing with their companions when Private R. Vince, age thirty-five, suddenly collapsed. His friends initially believed he was just drunk, but on further examination they realized he was in trouble and called for a doctor. The doctor examined Vince and declared him dead from a heart attack.[65]

In October 1917 Prohibition became law and the King Edward Hotel bar closed. In the spring of the following year Millington and Wolfenden sold the hotel to S.W. Hurst. With the bar revenue now gone, Hurst did the best he could to maintain the hotel over the following years, but in 1922 the hotel officially closed and became a rooming house.

EMPRESS HOTEL
1908

There were sophisticated, first-class hotels in Victoria long before the Empress Hotel opened in January 1908, but none could top the sheer magnificence and majesty of the Empress. What can I say about this grand lady, the elegant Empress Hotel, other than it is the greatest and most luxurious hotel ever built in Victoria?

Rumours that the Canadian Pacific Railway Company was considering building a tourist hotel in Victoria began circulating as early as 1901.[66] The front page of the *Colonist* for December 1, 1903, confirmed that Canadian Pacific would be building a substantial seven-storey building in Victoria, with many elaborate features suggestive of Château Frontenac in Quebec City. Included in the description of the hotel was an outline of the lower level, which would feature a German grill room, an adjoining billiards room, and a Turkish lounge complete with a bar and Turkish bath.[67]

In 1903 Francis Rattenbury, an architect with Canadian Pacific, suggested that the new hotel should be located on land reclaimed from James Bay, a centrepiece between the new legislative buildings and the post office on Government Street. This seemed a much better location than the existing plan, which was to build the hotel on the Douglas Gardens, a nine-acre tract of land located on the southeast corner of Government and Belleville Streets.[68] Rattenbury won the day, and the new Canadian Pacific tourist hotel was to be built on the reclaimed mudflats of James Bay, which became 721 Government Street.

Sir Thomas Shaughnessy, president of Canadian Pacific, stated that the new hotel would initially cost around $465,000. The main contract went to A.E. Barrett of Seattle, but a dozen other contractors supplied special materials, such as E.G. Prior & Company, which supplied the structural steel, and the Victoria brickmaker M. Humber & Sons, which supplied 2,750,000 bricks.[69] The Empress Hotel was granted a liquor licence in June 1906 for the planned German Grill Room and Turkish lounge bars, which were to open on the lower level. The Grill Room was equipped with a special oven and grill that came all the way

The German Grill and Tavern in the basement of the Empress Hotel.

from New York City. The bar in the Grill Room became the favourite haunt of politicians and members of the press gallery.

The Empress Hotel opened to the public on January 20, 1908, at the cost of $1 million, but it was worth it. The Empress was in a class by itself. Nothing even came close to the craftsmanship, excellent view of the harbour, and sheer magnificence of this seven-storey masterpiece.[70] The 1908 centre block is distinguished by its château-style roofline, steep slate roofs, neo-Gothic dormers and gables, and domed polygon turrets, making the hotel a recognizable landmark in the city.[71] The interior of the hotel was decorated in green and cream, with a touch of rust in the carpets throughout.

By the end of 1908 the Empress Hotel had taken in $80,000, and 1909 looked promising as the hotel was filled to capacity on a regular basis.[72] In fact, potential guests had to be turned away as the original 160 rooms filled quickly. A decision was made to add more rooms to the grand hotel. In December 1909, $200,000 was invested in a five-storey addition on the south side. When finished, the south wing added sixty-eight bedrooms and forty-eight baths.[73] In 1912 a ballroom and a library were added, designed by W.S. Painter; the library eventually became the Coronet Room and then the Bengal Lounge.[74] A much larger addition on the north wing would be completed in 1929.

Prohibition came to the Empress Hotel in October 1917 and, like at the other hotels, it did hurt the bottom line. The Empress bar was forced to close, and wine could no longer be served in the dining room. The once popular billiards room was refurbished in 1928 as the Georgian Lounge, which could be rented for private parties—one way to circumvent British

Columbia's strict liquor laws.[75] The German Grill Room became the alcohol-free Tudor Grill.

The Empress Hotel endured through the cycle of tough economic times, including Prohibition, and continued to prosper and grow into the fine world-class hotel it is today.

Through the 1860s to the 1910s Victoria's first-class hotels offered excellent service in an atmosphere of opulence. As the years went by, more first-class hotels were built, allowing travellers a wider choice. The sophistication and technology of the hotels improved, making Victoria a mecca for tourists. Victoria had a lot to offer: a mild climate, beautiful scenery, a quaint Englishness, and magnificent hotels, from the earliest high-class establishments, such as the St. Nicholas and the Driard House, to the final word in opulence, the grandest of them all, the Empress Hotel.

The decades between 1870 and 1899 are considered the golden age for saloons and hotel bars in Victoria. The sheer number of saloons during that period speaks to their popularity. This was the era when one could literally fall out of one saloon and hit another, as there were eighty-five licensed saloons and hotel bars in a city with a population of just over six thousand permanent residents. By the 1890s liquor consumption in British Columbia was nearly double the national average.[76] Chapter Four will take a look at the wide variety of hotels and hotel bars, as well as a selection of saloons, that plied their trade during the golden age when beer flowed like water and in most cases was considerably cheaper.

THE GOLDEN AGE

1870-99

The mouth of a perfectly happy man is filled with beer.

—Ancient Egyptian proverb, 2200 BC[1]

1. Rock Bay Hotel
2. Ship Inn (IV)
3. Belmont Saloon
4. Occidental Hotel
5. Grand Pacific Hotel
6. Klondike Hotel Bar

7. Horseshoe Saloon
8. Peter Steele's Saloon
9. Bismarck Saloon
10. Regent Saloon
11. Leland House (first location)
12. Leland House (second location)

S aloons and hotel bars always managed to have enough customers to sustain them through the boom-and-bust economy. This theory was tested during the worldwide depression of the 1870s, during which few merchants, aside from the barmen, did much business and bankruptcy was common.[2] Saloons and hotel bars had entered a golden age when almost everyone drank and many people drank to excess in an atmosphere with very few government restrictions.

The saloons filled up, especially on Saturday nights, when one could eat cheese and biscuits for free and wash it all down with a five-cent schooner of beer. The police blotter contained numerous references to arrests for public drunkenness and minor property damage.[3] There were more drunks arrested in Victoria than in any other place.[4] Punishment for public drunkenness was as follows: a small fine for the first offence, potential jail time for the second, and jail and time spent on the chain gang for the third. Countless stories go along with the arrests for public drunkenness. One story well worth mentioning is the case of Mrs. Murphy and her missing pet rooster.

One summer morning Mrs. Murphy went to feed her five-dollar Road Island Red rooster, only to find that it had been stolen. Evidence at the scene pointed to the theory that the bird had met with foul play. Mrs. Murphy notified Constable Hawton of the Victoria Police, who tracked the path of the thieves by following the feathers down Humboldt Street to a cabin just outside the White Horse Hotel. Inside he found the culprits, Johnny "Lager Beer" Wagner and George "Boozy" Hues, cooking the fat Road Island Red. They had been caught red-handed and were arrested on the spot. Both thieves were known to the police as notorious jailbirds who had recently completed a sentence from a previous conviction of public drunkenness.[5] Both were found guilty of theft. Lager Beer Wagner was sentenced to one month in jail, while Boozy Hues avoided a lengthy jail term and hard labour on the understanding that he would leave Victoria, as "prison authorities were growing tired of having him as a boarder," and seek fresh fields and pastures new, where chickens were more plentiful and the law was not so stringent.[6]

Aside from the sheer stupidity of a handful of saloon patrons, the mix of American capital and British law and order worked. The small yet resourceful Victoria Police Department usually got their man and the streets were relatively safe. The automobile had not yet been invented, so drinking and driving was not a concern, although there were a few problems with the odd coachman who, after waiting for hours outside the bars for a customer, would have a few too many himself and occasionally lose control of his hack.

By the 1880s technology was improving. Electricity replaced gas, allowing for much brighter street lights, which were appreciated during the long, dark winters; electricity also proved much safer than gas or oil. By 1887 the Victoria and Esquimalt Telephone Company reported that there were 350 phones in use. And on February 22, 1890, the National Electric Tramway and Lighting Company introduced the first electric streetcar in

Victoria.[7] Three more streetcars went into service later that year on four miles of track.

On March 29, 1888, an extension of the Esquimalt and Nanaimo (E&N) Railway was completed in Victoria by coal baron Robert Dunsmuir. The downtown hotels profited from Victoria's position, at Store Street, as the southern terminus of the E&N railroad line. In 1896 the Victoria to Sidney line would open, and in 1905 the E&N was extended northward to Courtenay. Rail service made it much faster to transport people and goods, which in turn brought the costs of transportation down.

The 1890s began with the outbreak of a smallpox epidemic followed by a worldwide depression. The sealing industry, which began back in the 1860s, was in decline due to stiff competition from the Americans and Russians and a worldwide glut of product in the marketplace. The failing seal market affected the hotels, as most sealing captains and their crews would stay in Victoria's hotels and spend money in the bars and saloons during the off-season.

The economy came roaring back when gold was discovered in the Yukon Territory in 1896. In August of that year a steamer arrived in Seattle carrying prospectors who had struck it rich near Dawson City in the Klondike. Gold was being mined at a place called Rabbit Creek (later known as Bonanza Creek) and at a number of other creeks in the Yukon. The Klondike Gold Rush began in late 1896, and by 1899 most of the gold had been mined. During that time, more than one hundred thousand gold seekers set out for the goldfields, though only thirty thousand actually made it. Of those two thousand found some gold, and about fifty struck it rich. Dawson City was nicknamed "Paris of the North,"[8] and the Klondike Gold Rush provided the impetus for the economy to get on its feet again all along the west coast of North America. In Victoria new businesses sprung up overnight with names celebrating the gold rush, like the Dawson Hotel, the Klondike Saloon, Klondike Outfitters, and the Klondike Mining and Trading Company.

The old century was ending on a positive note and the new century promised to be an era of prosperity, especially in Victoria. On February 10, 1898, the spectacular new Parliament Buildings opened, and there was talk of the Canadian Pacific Railway Company building a deluxe hotel in the city. Technology was making life easier, and there was excitement and optimism about the future.

The bar business was never better or busier. The sheer number and variety of saloons and hotel bars reached a climax during this time—it was truly their golden age. There were dark clouds on the horizon, but everyone was having too good of a time to notice.

ROCK BAY HOTEL
1863–1917

The Rock Bay House opened between the bridges on the northwest corner of Work (now Bay) and Bridge Streets in 1863, with J.W. Cromer as proprietor. Rock Bay was a small community northwest of Victoria that was considered part of Esquimalt at the time, as the Point Ellice Bridge connected to the west. Rock Bay was nothing like the light industrial area it is today. One hundred and fifty

The Rock Bay Hotel, northwest corner of Bay and Bridge Streets.

years ago it was nestled in a very pleasant rural setting with roads lined with fruit trees and a few scattered residential houses. The pace of life was slow and easy and everyone knew their neighbour.

The Rock Bay House was a modest wood structure that offered clean rooms, a well-stocked bar, meals at all hours from the restaurant, and a bowling alley. Bowling was almost as popular as billiards, and a few saloons and hotels built in that special feature to attract customers. Patrons would enjoy a drink and puff away at their cigars while bowling a few frames.

In October 1863 William Hartley sold the Rock Bay Tannery and purchased the Rock Bay House from Cromer. It wasn't long before the new proprietor landed himself in hot water with the law. Hartley was accused of selling whisky to an Aboriginal person, and the penalty, if found guilty, was a fine of twenty pounds (the currency in use at the time) or two months' imprisonment. The judge remarked that he regretted that such a fine, respectable man as William Hartley should have to go through this ordeal, but that all dealers convicted of whisky trafficking must face the highest penalty of the law.[9]

There is no further record of the Rock Bay House until 1867, when George Kerry Booth was the proprietor. It appears that Booth had the same bad luck as Hartley. In August 1867 Booth appeared before a judge, charged with harbouring deserters. After a lengthy examination, Booth was convicted of the crime. He lashed out violently when the guilty verdict was read in court, denouncing the decision and claiming his innocence. He was thrown in jail for twenty-four hours for contempt of court.[10]

In May 1873 the City of Victoria passed the Additional Taverns License By-Law, which stated that saloons and hotels that sold liquor within the new extended city limits of Beacon Hill, Cedar Hill, and Rock Bay were to pay thirty-five dollars each for a six-month licence. The law applied to the Park Hotel, the Lion Tap Saloon, the Bridge Saloon, and the Rock Bay House.

George Booth sold the Rock Bay House in 1874. Over the next fourteen years, seven proprietors came and went. By 1888 Ross J. Ferguson owned the Rock Bay House, and he was there to see it burn to the ground the following year.[11] Unfortunately, there is no account of the fire in the *Colonist*, but a brief account from the Victoria Fire Department noted that four wooden buildings were completely destroyed by fire, including the Rock Bay House, Wrightman's grocery store, and the Woodbine Cottage, which were over a mile from the nearest fire hall.[12] In March 1889 Ferguson asked that the licence for the Rock Bay House, recently destroyed by the fire, be transferred to Mr. Booth, but his request was denied.[13] Meanwhile, the lot sat empty for months until it was purchased by Alexander Cameron in 1891.

Seeing the need for a hotel in the area, Cameron had the new Rock Bay Hotel built. The three-storey brick hotel was designed by Cornelius John Soule in June 1891 and opened in November. The hotel offered forty guest rooms, a large parlour, three sitting rooms, offices, baths, and a barroom—but no bowling alley.[14] Cameron applied for a liquor licence in November 1891, but was refused. He tried again a number of times in 1892, unsuccessfully, until he finally granted a three-month licence in February 1893. Cameron would lease his hotel out for months at a time, come back and run it for a while, then lease it out again. He continued this practice until he sold the hotel in 1898 at the height of the Klondike Gold Rush.

F.J. Brock purchased the Rock Bay Hotel and reopened it in

Heaney Company and the fourth version of the Ship Inn Saloon, 1217 Wharf Street, ca. 1900.
IMAGE #H-02671 COURTESY OF THE ROYAL BC MUSEUM AND ARCHIVES

September 1898. Brock refurbished the rooms and updated the bar, hiring J.H. Chambers as head bartender. Once Brock paid the money to update the hotel, he put it up for sale. From 1899 to 1908 the hotel changed hands five times until Bertram A. Holden bought it. Holden brought some stability to the old hostelry, successfully running the business for five years. Rooms cost four dollars per month and upward, board was four dollars per week, and beds went for twenty-five cents a night.

A tragic event took place in the backyard of the Rock Bay Hotel one summer evening in 1904. Joseph Bailey, former proprietor of the Occidental Hotel at Wharf and Johnson Streets and of the Halfway House in Esquimalt, attempted to commit suicide by cutting his throat with a razor. His cries of anguish were heard inside the bar, and it was later learned that Bailey was despondent over his recent separation from his wife.[15]

In June 1908 Holden put the hotel up for sale. Partners James Hogg and J. Rae purchased the hotel and operated it until it closed in 1922. The old hotel sat vacant for years until it was purchased and renovated into the Rock Bay Apartments in 1933. The building was torn down and replaced in 1995.

SHIP INN (IV)
1868–1913

James Strachan and James Mady opened the fourth version of the Ship Inn Saloon at (81) 1217 Wharf Street in 1868. James Yates had built the first Ship Inn in 1851 and its replacement in 1860 (both of which were located on Wharf Street). The third Ship Inn was in Esquimalt. Strachan and Mady also ran the Market Exchange Saloon on Fort Street. Within a year the two agreed to part ways, and the partnership was dissolved. Mady carried on business at the Market Exchange and Strachan became the sole owner of the Ship Inn.

The Ship Inn was a typical working-class saloon: small, with a long bar, a few tables, a small kitchen, and a bathroom. It also offered hot lunches and a quiet card room.

James Strachan was born in Scotland around 1810. After immigrating to the United States, he eventually made his home in San Francisco. He moved to Victoria in the early 1860s, and by 1863 he was a successful liquor merchant on Wharf Street. In 1871 he suffered a paralytic stroke, which affected his ability to walk and caused his health to go on a steady decline.[16] Around that same time, Strachan invested in a whale oil company with a man named Douglass, his new business partner and a fellow Scot. The company was short-lived, but it did manage to produce fifteen thousand gallons of oil in 1871. The following March saw the company close and sell off its assets at auction.[17] The Ship Inn provided a steady income for Strachan, which allowed him to dabble in the market and invest in all sorts of ventures. Some were more promising than others. In March 1881 Strachan received bad news regarding an investment in which he lost a large sum of money. That was the end of James Strachan.

Mr. Richard Jones was strolling along the beach at the foot of Menzies Street in James Bay when he saw what looked like a body in the water. Realizing it was a human being, Jones waded out and brought the unfortunate person to shore. He recognized the deceased man as James Strachan of the Ship Inn Saloon. It was determined later that the late Mr. Strachan had left his home at about eleven o'clock the preceding morning and had been seen passing Government Square toward Menzies Street, and it was remarked how weak and forlorn he had appeared. He had reportedly received a letter by mail concerning some business that was not satisfactory, and it was supposed that he had gone down to the beach, waded into the water, and drowned himself.[18] Those who knew Strachan well, however, were not so sure that he had committed suicide, as Strachan was known to wash his feet in the salty water to get some relief. They reasoned that Strachan, partially crippled from his stroke, had lost his balance while washing his feet and had fallen into the water and drowned. No inquest into the details of his death took place.[19]

Samuel Sea—an appropriate name for the proprietor of a place called the Ship Inn—looked after the affairs of the saloon while it was for sale. It was purchased by John Bartlett, the bartender at the Brown Jug Saloon. In 1887 the Ship Inn passed to another bartender, Charlie McCluskey, formerly of the Grotto Saloon on Government Street. The following eight years saw four proprietors come and go at the Ship Inn. In 1894 George Thompson was running the establishment.

In a strange twist of fate, the new proprietor of the saloon had been on the job for only a few weeks before he too succumbed to drowning. The seventy-year-old publican was found floating face down in Victoria Harbour at six o'clock in the morning by two crew members on the ship *Joan*.[20] During the inquest that followed his death, it came to light that he was despondent over the loss of his best friend and complained that business at his new saloon was not as good as he had hoped.

Then there are the bizarre stories that came out of the Ship Inn. One Saturday evening the fourteen jail cells in the city lock-up filled up with sixteen "guests" who were arrested for various minor charges, the most common being drunk in public. An interesting exception was the thief who was apprehended at the Ship Inn and charged with stealing ladies' underwear and a handful of ostrich feathers.[21]

The Ship Inn was not a particularly rowdy saloon, and fights between patrons were rare—with one bloody exception. On a pleasant summer evening in 1911, George Stefano and Joseph Pedro were sitting at a table in the Ship Inn, talking and enjoying a beer, when G. Goispino (alias "Patchy"), from Jordan River, and his companion, Petro Stridiato, entered the saloon. A few hours went by, with all four men getting drunk. Suddenly a squabble broke out between the two groups. That is when Patchy approached Stefano and Pedro from behind and produced an empty whisky bottle from his jacket, which he proceeded to smash over the head of the unsuspecting Stefano. Then Patchy wasted no time in sticking the jagged bottle into Pedro's neck and head, causing him to bleed profusely. The bartender leapt into action, grabbing the broken bottle out of the hands of Patchy and then immediately calling the police. Patchy and his friend Stridiato disappeared into the night, but Stridiato was soon found and arrested. Patchy got away and was never seen again. Stefano was sent to the hospital and Pedro was attended to by a doctor in the bar. Both recovered from their ordeal.[22]

In December 1913 Angelo Doria, the last proprietor of the Ship Inn Saloon, was forced to close the bar. Doria applied to have the licence transferred to the London Cafe at 705 Johnson Street. The Ship Inn Saloon had been in business for forty-five years.

BELMONT SALOON
1871–1912

The unpretentious two-storey wooden Belmont Saloon began as the John Bull Saloon in 1859. It was built on the northeast corner of (11) 801 Government and (2) 602 Humboldt Streets and lasted fifty-three years (it was pulled down and replaced with the Belmont Office Building in 1912). William Craswell reopened the old John Bull Saloon in 1871, updating it and renaming it the Belmont Saloon. Craswell was an experienced hotelman, having run the Island Hotel on Government Street with his partner, C.B. Brown, from 1862 to 1864. Craswell liked the location of the old John Bull Saloon and thought, with some basic improvements, that the saloon would provide him with a decent living. Craswell notified the public that the old place was open again under his management and that the bar was ready to "supply families by the case or by the bottle."[23]

Craswell ran the saloon for about a year before selling it to Jarvis Longhurst. As it would turn out, Longhurst was the longest-serving proprietor of the Belmont Saloon, operating it for nineteen years as the sole proprietor, from 1872 until 1891, and for a further nine years in partnership with the Flewins to 1900. "Ask your friends to take a drink and try Jarvis Longhurst's Belmont Saloon," read the advertisements in the *Colonist*.[24]

Jarvis Longhurst was born August 3, 1830, in the small hamlet of Hartley in the southeast corner of England. On March 3, 1850, Longhurst set off from his homeland, eventually arriving in Victoria aboard the SS *Tory* on May 9, 1851.

When not tending to the bar in his Belmont Saloon, Longhurst was frequently seen down by the harbour. His favourite hobby was aquatic sports, from sculling to sailing. Longhurst owned the twenty-foot sailboat *Mary*, which he loved to race. He regularly raced his boat from the James Bay Bridge "and around the bell buoy twice" inside Victoria Harbour against Mr. Jones and his boat *Photograph*.[25] A healthy competition between Longhurst and Jones developed and would last for years. Each year they would race for bragging rights and vie for the Silver Cup trophy. When Longhurst won, the Silver Cup was proudly displayed in a glass case inside the Belmont Saloon, and when he didn't win, the case sat empty for that year. Regular customers learned not to talk about sailboat racing if they noticed the trophy case was empty. Longhurst would host sailing competitions in which interested parties would sign up and pay their twenty-five-dollar entrance fee at his saloon. Eventually, Longhurst's love of competitive sailing would attract crews from Puget Sound and San Francisco, and large sums of money would be wagered on the outcomes of these races.

Perhaps Longhurst wanted to spend more time on his boat, because in 1891 he took on two partners, brothers William H. and Albert Charles Flewin, to help run the Belmont Saloon. Meanwhile, business was brisk in the Belmont bar as it was a popular destination for seafarers, sportsmen, and blue-collar barflies.

The Flewin brothers were born in Victoria. Their father,

The Belmont Saloon, on the northeast corner of
Government and Humboldt Streets, ca. 1905.
ARTWORK BY GORDON FRIESEN, 2015

Thomas Flewin, had emigrated from Kent, England, and had opened the Capital Saloon at (7) Yates Street on June 15, 1882. William, the younger brother, worked at the Belmont Tannery for years before getting into the saloon business. He was twenty years old when he married Ada Botterell, and they had several children together. William's term as co-proprietor of the Belmont Saloon did not last long, as he died on November 25, 1899, at the age of thirty-seven.

When William Flewin died, Albert Flewin and Jarvis Longhurst decided to sell the Belmont Saloon. On March 13, 1900, Peter Wolf became the new proprietor. Albert Flewin went on to run his father's Capital Saloon, until his death in 1902. Longhurst, in his seventies, eventually moved to Duncan and ran the Quamichan Hotel. He lived a long and fulfilling life and died in 1921 at the ripe old age of ninety.

Wolf sold the Belmont Hotel property to a Winnipeg firm in September 1903, but stayed on with the saloon under lease until 1905, when he sold the lease to John Morgan. Morgan, with his brother James Morgan as head bartender, ran the Belmont Saloon until it closed in 1911. John Morgan was a tough, hard-working man who had survived the loss of a leg while a mate on a river steamer during the Klondike Gold Rush.[26] It was during Morgan's tenure that some of the more interesting events occurred at the Belmont.

One spring day in 1908, customers were enjoying their drinks in the Belmont Saloon when two constables came in and grabbed a man sitting at the bar. He fit the description of a suspect who had attempted to burn down Spencer's Department Store earlier in the day.[27] In another incident, a man was found badly beaten and bleeding on Government Street. Apparently he and an acquaintance had been drinking heavily in the Belmont Saloon when they got into an argument that turned quite nasty.[28]

Perhaps the most disturbing incident that occurred around this time was when Walter Gossop, a well-known character in town, attempted to kill himself inside the Belmont Saloon. Gossop was quite inebriated when he suddenly pulled out a pen-knife and began cutting his throat. If it were not for the quick actions of the bartender, Gossop would have succeeded in committing suicide. The police were summoned, and while in custody Gossop attempted to end his life twice more. He was restrained pending his transfer to the asylum in New Westminster. It was generally believed that Gossop, once a successful schoolteacher, had become "mentally affected by drink."[29]

By 1908 the neighbourhood was changing. The grand Empress Hotel opened in January. It, along with the Parliament Buildings and post office buildings, completed a trio of impressive new structures that reflected the British Empire at the height of its power and prestige. The Belmont Saloon was dwarfed by these monoliths of the new Edwardian age; the old wooden saloon looked out of place, and it was just a matter of time before it would be demolished. Negotiations were under way as early as 1909 to sell the saloon to a group of investors who had plans to tear the old building down and replace it with "a handsome six-storey structure that would be comprised of offices and apartments."[30] The new building would be named the Belmont Block.

By the summer of 1911 a deal was struck between the developers of the Belmont Block and the owners of the Belmont Saloon from Winnipeg. In August 1911 Morgan, the proprietor of the saloon, announced that a farewell luncheon would take place at the Belmont. The saloon was packed for the occasion, and a farewell toast was made to honour the fifty-two years of the Belmont and its predecessor, the John Bull Saloon. In June 1912 Morgan attempted to transfer the liquor licence to new premises, but the application was refused due to the fact that the Belmont Saloon no longer existed. The saloon was demolished and the liquor licence was allowed to lapse.

OCCIDENTAL HOTEL
1877–1925

There were five Occidental Hotels on the west coast in the 1870s. Two were in Victoria, one in New Westminster, one in San Francisco, and one in a small coastal town just south of the border called Seattle. The Occidental Hotel that we are about to look at was located on Wharf Street near Johnson Street in Victoria.

William Jensen arrived in Victoria on a Puget Sound steamer from Seattle. He bought the old Royal Hotel—the second brick building in town, built in 1858—remodelled it, and renamed it the Occidental Hotel. The hotel opened on November 7, 1877.

The Occidental Hotel offered sixty rooms at a cost of twenty-five cents a bed for the night. Board and lodging for a week cost six dollars, and single meals went for twenty-five cents. The hotel also had a spacious bar, parlours, and a dining room. Jensen's hotel was situated in an excellent location just across Wharf Street from the docks, making it very convenient for guests arriving and departing by ship from or to the Fraser River, Puget Sound, or California. Later, when the E&N Railway line was completed, its southern terminus went practically to the front door of the Occidental Hotel. Viewing the hotel from outside the front door, one couldn't miss the twelve impressive chimneys and the second-floor wraparound balcony.

Shortly after the hotel opened, a guest met with a terrible fate. William Joe Rice, a real estate agent, arrived from San Francisco, spent hours in the bar, then left and was seen staggering around the docks. He fell into the harbour and drowned.[31] In spite of that tragic accident, Jensen did not have a problem renewing his liquor licence, as the Commissioner of Licenses stated that a bar was part and parcel of running a hotel.[32]

In the spring of 1882 Jensen purchased the properties north of his hotel to the corner of Wharf and Johnson Streets and two buildings east on Johnson Street in order to expand the hotel. The properties had a number of small dilapidated wooden buildings, which Jensen had removed. He commissioned popular architect John Teague to design a two-storey brick addition to his hotel.

The new Occidental Hotel opened in the summer of 1882 with added frontage of fifty-five feet on Wharf Street to the corner with Johnson Street, where an additional one hundred feet stretched along the south side close to Waddington Street. The handsome two-storey Occidental boasted a beautiful, wide oak staircase to the seventy-six rooms on the spacious second floor. Each room had an abundance of natural light and an excellent view. Two large stores, a number of offices, and sitting rooms were added to the ground floor, and the dining room was enlarged and refitted. The Occidental bar and billiards room was to become

The Occidental Hotel, southeast corner of Wharf and Johnson Streets.

one of the most famous on the coast, noted in part for providing thirsty customers with "Ye Olde XXXX eight-year-old imported ale" on tap. In December 1888 the Occidental Hotel, along with the nearby California Hotel and the Colonial Hotel, was fitted with electric lights.

In March 1889 a thief broke into the Occidental bar through a window and stole ten dollars from the till and a bottle of whisky. The burglar was one of a gang of five robbers who had gone on a crime spree that night. All were caught and prosecuted.[33] The Occidental bar was the target of another theft in which thirty dollars was taken from the till and a few bottles of whisky and a box of cigars were stolen. Joe Williams, who had a string of aliases and was wanted for theft in Seattle, was arrested and charged with six counts of burglary.[34]

During the late 1880s, William Jensen was a busy man, dividing his time between the Occidental and the Dallas, as well as managing the Dawson. In November 1895 Jensen had the Occidental Hotel totally refitted and modernized. He then sold the Occidental to Walter H. Porter in October 1896. This ended Jensen's long and productive time as the owner of the hotel he had created and worked so hard to improve throughout the years into one of the leading hotels in Victoria. Jensen refused to retire, instead lending his experience to owning and operating the Sidney Hotel, which he did successfully for many years.

An unsettling incident took place at the Occidental Hotel in the summer of 1902. A couple was strolling along the sidewalk outside the hotel when a body fell out of the sky and landed a few feet in front of them. Rushing to the limp body to render aid, the shocked couple noticed that it was that of an unconscious woman.

A doctor was summoned and the injured woman was taken inside the hotel and examined. She had a broken wrist and lacerations on one leg. The doctor saw that she had been beaten about the face, injuries most likely received before she was thrown out of the second-storey hotel window.[35] The facts of the case came out in court. It appeared that the woman and an acquaintance named Johnny had been sharing a bottle of whisky when Johnny had begun to make unwanted advances toward her; when she refused him, he became violent. Johnny had beaten her, and in a fit of rage had thrown her out of the window. Johnny drew a lengthy prison term for his actions.

The Occidental Hotel continued to prosper through a succession of proprietors up to 1910. Theodore Anderson managed the hotel from 1910 until Prohibition in 1917. The hotel went through a substantial refurbishment in January 1914, contracted to builders Dinsdale and Malcolm at the cost of $2,000.[36] That was the last major renovation of the hotel before Prohibition shut down the bar.

The Occidental Hotel struggled on without the bar revenue for a few years, but it became run down and soon earned a reputation as a seedy place and a haven for prostitutes. In 1925 the once extraordinary hotel closed.

GRAND PACIFIC HOTEL
1879–1916

There has been a saloon on the northeast corner of Store and Johnson Streets since the pioneer days. By 1860 the Lager Beer

The Grand Pacific Hotel in 1883, northeast corner of Johnson and Store Streets.
IMAGE #A-02719 COURTESY OF THE ROYAL BC MUSEUM AND ARCHIVES

Saloon was in that location, "where will be found the best of everything for the refreshment of the inner man." [37] Giacomo Bossi, with his brother Carlo, built the Grand Pacific Hotel at (26) 530 Johnson Street in 1879.

The Italian Bossi brothers were major players during the early building boom and were well known in Victoria society. Both brothers held significant properties around town; they commissioned Italianate masonry structures at 516 and 522 Johnson Street and at 1435 and 1455 Store Street, as well as a commercial building at 529 Cormorant (now Pandora) Street. [38]

The sixty-room Grand Pacific Hotel was a beautiful yet frugal three-storey Italianate building that developed over time with a series of in-style additions in 1883 and 1887. The building featured ornamental window hoods and an overhanging cornice supported by intricate scroll-cut paired brackets. The R.T. Williams directory for 1882–83 described Bossi's new hotel as "undoubtedly one of the handsomest buildings in the city." [39] Inside the thirty-by-thirty-foot hotel bar, located on the ground floor on the Store Street side, Bossi installed the "longest bar in town," where customers could enjoy dark pints of beer for five cents each. [40] A corner door in the bar allowed access from both Johnson and Store Streets, while on the other side of the barroom a door led out into a hall and to a staircase to the rooms above.

In 1883 the hotel was extended eastward, maintaining the same Italianate style originally used in 1879 and allowing the Grand Pacific to offer a total of eighty-one well-furnished rooms. The Bossi brothers retained ownership of the building but leased it out to David M. Ellis in January 1884, as they had their hands full with building and operating their other properties. Ellis had considerable experience in the hotel industry, having operated the Orleans Hotel on the corner of Store and Cormorant (now Pandora) Streets from 1878 to 1880. Then he ran the Commercial Hotel from 1880 to 1884 until he became the proprietor at the Grand Pacific.

Like the Occidental Hotel, which was kitty-corner from the Grand Pacific, the location of the hostelry could not have been better. It was only steps away from the steamboat wharves, and the new E&N Railway's southern terminus was located just west of the hotel. Business was booming and all was well until disaster struck in April 1885.

A fire broke out at the Terminus Hotel on Johnson Street near the Grand Pacific, and fuelled by increasing winds, it was soon out of control. The fire consumed the frail wood structures along Johnson Street running both east and west until it reached the Grand Pacific Hotel.

"The fire was now next to the Grand Pacific where the cornice and windows soon burst out in a mass of flames. As the fire increased men ran to all the rooms and alerted lodgers, furniture and effects were next once the people were out of harm's way."[41] The quick actions of the two Victoria Fire Departments, the Tiger and the Deluge, saved the Grand Pacific Hotel, although the upper floors were badly burned and there was water damage throughout. Initially it was believed that nobody had been killed or seriously hurt in the massive fire, but it was later learned that an unidentified Chinese man and Charlie Anderson, the coach driver for the Terminus Hotel, had been killed in the blaze. Total monetary losses came to over $25,000. Fortunately, both hotels were fully insured and Mr. Ellis received a cheque to cover the fire losses within four days of the disaster.

The old Grand Pacific Hotel building in 2016.
PHOTOGRAPH BY PETE KOHUT

David Ellis had to give up his lease due to poor health, and owner Giacomo Bossi took over the management of the hotel for a few years. On September 22, 1888, the Veterans of the American Civil War held a banquet at the Grand Pacific Hotel. American veterans arriving at the hotel were welcomed by a huge Old Glory flying proudly from the highest point on the roof of the hotel. Bossi had installed the large American flag to honour the veterans and to celebrate the anniversary.

Bossi advertised that his hotel was again up for lease. From March 1890 to 1896 the hotel went through three proprietors. Carlo Bossi returned briefly in 1896 to operate the Grand Pacific, but he died in November 1896.

Lorenzo Reda managed the Grand Pacific Hotel from 1897 to 1908. The hotel's final addition expanded it eastward in 1897, an expense that the hotel could certainly afford at the time. The hotel and its bar were doing a good business, especially from the activities brought on by the Klondike Gold Rush. The bar patrons could get rowdy at times, but serious troubles were few—except for one incident that attracted the police. A local regular at the bar, Charles Miller, pulled out a concealed pistol during an argument with another man. For that act Miller was arrested, and when found guilty he was ordered to pay a twenty-two-dollar fine.[42]

On another occasion, a guest at the hotel named William Anderson was making for Victoria and the Grand Pacific Hotel when he had his blankets and a few suitcases stolen along the way. After checking into his room, he spent some time in the hotel bar. He woke with a heavy head the next day, and when he came to his senses he discovered that thirty-five dollars were missing.

Anderson was certainly down on his luck; he claimed the money had been stolen by a woman he was with that night, but he lost the case in court due to lack of evidence.[43]

The most talked-about confrontation that took place in the bar at the Grand Pacific Hotel, however, was the stabbing of Joe and Louis Palosa. The bar was packed with regular customers who frequented the place most afternoons: labourers, long-shoremen, cabinetmakers, and brick and stone masons—most of Italian descent—drinking beer and whisky. The bartender, Eugene Boccaccio, had just served the Palosa brothers while they and other patrons were singing. Tony Reda, brother to the proprietor Lorenzo Reda, did not care for their singing and told them to "shut up." An argument ensued that quickly escalated into a fight. Punches were thrown, and just as quickly as the melee had begun, it ended, with Louis and Joe Palosa lying on the floor, both bleeding from stab wounds inflicted by Tony Reda, who bolted for the door and was gone. Reda was known as a hothead who had been in trouble before, attacking a man with an axe on one occasion and threatening a man with a gun on another. The Palosa brothers were taken to Jubilee Hospital, where Louis's injuries were found to be quite grave. Doctors did not expect that he would recover, but his brother, Joe, had sustained much less serious wounds. Meanwhile, the police followed a trail of blood left by the fleeing Reda, and he was soon apprehended and sent to jail to await trial for attempted murder.[44]

A few days following the fracas, an interesting follow-up to the story appeared in the *Colonist*: "The victim [Louis Palosa] of the affray now seems likely to disappoint the doctors and recover, in the face of their prediction that he could not possibly do so. When first taken to the hospital he was given less than twenty-four hours to live—yet he is still alive, and what is more, reported to show signs of continued improvement."[45] In spite of the "disappointment" of the doctors, Louis Palosa survived the knife attack and, along with his brother Joe, testified in court, which eventually resulted in the conviction of Tony Reda.

In 1908 Lorenzo Reda sold the Grand Pacific Hotel lease to Virginio Bargetto, who was the last proprietor of the hotel. By 1916 the old hostelry was showing her age, so Bargetto and his partner, Riamendo Milanesio, spent a considerable sum to improve the hotel and specifically the hotel bar. But in November 1916 Bargetto had a run-in with the liquor licensing commission that led to the end of the Grand Pacific Hotel.

In November 1916 Bargetto served a mickey of rum during the bar's off-hours to P.C. Phillips, who turned out to be an undercover policeman. When Bargetto learned who Phillips was, he attempted to bribe the constable with twenty dollars. The case went to court, and Bargetto was convicted of selling liquor after hours and attempting to bribe an officer. In his defence, Bargetto, a married man with children, who up until then hadn't had a police record, explained that the new restrictive hours and the recent great expense of refitting the bar had put him in a position of desperation, and he had made the wrong decision. The proprietors told the judge that the business was in jeopardy and that there was a real likelihood that they would have to close. The judge fined Bargetto $100 and warned that the bar would remain under tight scrutiny in the future.[46]

That was the last straw for Bargetto and Milanesio. After

paying the fine, they decided to let the remaining time on their liquor licence lapse and then close the bar and the hotel. The owners sold the Grand Pacific in March 1917 to a Japanese group not related to the hotel industry.

FOUR SALOONS
1891–1913

KLONDIKE HOTEL BAR, 1891–1912

John Draut opened the BC Grocery and Bakery on the southwest corner of Johnson and Blanshard Streets in 1880. By 1891 Draut had realized there was great potential for profit in running a saloon. He applied for a retail liquor licence and converted his store into a saloon. By 1898 the Klondike Gold Rush was in full swing, so he changed the name of his saloon to celebrate the occasion. In June 1912 Max Leiser purchased the building, and in September of that year, with his manager F.W. Kostenbader, he demolished it in order to erect a new hotel called the Kaiserhof (featured in Chapter Five).

HORSESHOE SALOON, 1899–1913

This saloon opened as the Nickel Plate Saloon in 1887 at (85) 1223 Government Street. In 1899 C.P. Le Lievre became the proprietor and changed the name to the Horseshoe Saloon, where one could enjoy a hardy helping of "beef tea and Oyster cocktails."[47] The saloon was forced to close in December 1913.

The Klondike Saloon, southwest corner of Blanshard and Johnson Streets.
IMAGE #D-03624 COURTESY OF THE ROYAL BC MUSEUM AND ARCHIVES

The Horseshoe Saloon, 1223 Government Street.
IMAGE #D-05587 COURTESY OF THE ROYAL BC MUSEUM AND ARCHIVES

Peter Steele's Saloon, 4 Bastion Square, 1902.
IMAGE #E-01555 COURTESY OF THE ROYAL BC MUSEUM AND ARCHIVES

Soldiers standing outside the Bismarck Saloon, 1303 Government Street, ca. 1912.
GLEN A. MOFFORD COLLECTION

PETER STEELE'S SALOON, 1899–1913

Peter Steele's Saloon and lunch room was located at 508 Bastion Street. Customers could enjoy a hot bowl of clam chowder and wash it down with a mug of Bass pure pale ale. A restaurant attached to the saloon served patrons from 7 AM to 7 PM. Steele also provided customers in the bar with English ales and stouts from the Stanley Park Brewery in Vancouver.[48]

BISMARCK SALOON, 1907–13

The Bismarck Saloon was located at (103) 1303 Government Street beside the Imperial Bank of Canada. John Abernethy Wallis changed the name from the Tourist Cafe to the Bismarck Saloon and operated it with bartenders George North and Jas Grigor. Samuel "Sam" Shore ran the saloon from 1908 to 1912. Shore's wife was the only fatality of the massive Five Sisters Block fire of 1910.

REGENT SALOON
1887–1913

If a vote had been held in the 1880s to determine which saloon was the most raucous in Victoria, the Regent Saloon on the southwest corner of Johnson and (96) 1328 Douglas Streets would have won hands down. (Or should I say hands up, due to the frequency of robberies that took place there?) The police received more calls to the notorious Regent Saloon than to any other drinking hole in town.

The two-storey wooden building that would eventually house the Regent Saloon was built in 1882 for grocer and liquor merchant Thomas Nicholson. In August 1883 a fight took place inside Nicholson's store in which Irishman Davie D. Lavin had a punch-up with Johnston Robertson. Lavin landed a solid right to Robertson's head and dropped him to the floor. Robertson's injuries were serious and he ended up in the hospital, where he died three days later. Lavin was arrested for manslaughter, but he claimed self-defence and was acquitted.[49] It was an ominous omen of things to come.

Ross Ferguson bought the business in 1886 and refitted it into the Regent Saloon. Ferguson ran the saloon at street level, while Barney Levy's cigar factory, where his crew rolled "Pride of Victoria" cigars, was situated on the second floor.

It was barely a year before Ferguson sold the Regent Saloon to George Connor and Henry Nicholson. Connor lasted a couple of years before he was forced to retire due to poor health; his partner, Nicholson, sold the saloon to John Switzer and Charles McClusky. In 1892 the old wooden structure was pulled down and replaced with a two-storey brick building. It was during the 1890s and into the early 1900s that the Regent earned its reputation as one of the rowdiest saloons in town, to the joy and entertainment of some but to the constant irritation of the police.

On April 4, 1891, a Mr. C. Winterhalter was charged with robbing the contents of the saloon's safe. The judge threw the case out due to lack of evidence and the fact that the only eyewitness was "dead drunk" at the time.[50] In 1900 the proprietor of the Regent Saloon was charged with selling beer on election day even

The building that once housed the Regent Saloon,
southwest corner of Douglas and Johnson Streets.
PHOTOGRAPH BY PETE KOHUT, 2016

though saloons were ordered shut until the polls closed. It was later learned that the bartender had sold ginger beer. When the polls finally closed, a group of men arrived at the Regent Saloon, and it wasn't long before a heated argument broke out over the preliminary results of the election. Jack Hayes, the proprietor of the Louvre Hotel, was so angry that he pulled out a concealed revolver from his coat and threatened to end the argument by ending the other man's life.[51]

One of my favourite stories from the Regent Saloon is this: Mr. B. Marmaas testified that he was having a quiet drink when he became the victim of an unprovoked attack by the defendant V. Steemeeteere. The defendant attacked with a "long and ugly looking knife," but Marmaas quickly grabbed a cuspidor at his feet and hit Steemeeteere on the head with it, spilling its contents at the same time. The bartender and an independent witness told a different story, saying that it was Marmaas who was the aggressor, having sucker-punched Steemeeteere for no apparent reason. That is when Steemeeteere showed Marmaas his intimidating knife, which was not hidden, and warned Marmaas to back off. Tempers appeared to cool down as both men continued drinking without further trouble. But when Steemeeteere left for home, he was promptly followed by Marmaas, who grabbed a cuspidor on his way out the door and used it to whack the unsuspecting Steemeeteere on the back of his head.[52] The fight continued out in the street and lasted until the police arrived.

Proprietors at the Regent Saloon didn't seem to last for more than two years. Perhaps it was because the place acted like a magnet for every tough and bully in town. It was simply too dangerous.

In 1908 William "Bill" Anderson bought the troubled Regent Saloon. Customers soon learned that Anderson was not a man to toy with. Anderson was a no-nonsense Scotsman from Aberdeen. He was also an ex-policeman and was the weight-throwing champion of California from 1885 to 1890. Anderson was a big man and he still maintained his athletic figure.[53] You would think his presence at the bar would have calmed things down, but he appears to have encouraged fighting. Whenever a fracas broke out—which was usually daily, and twice on Saturday nights—there Anderson would be, jumping in as referee or at times joining in the melee.

It wasn't always an animal show at the Regent, just more often than not. Anderson did erect a bulletin board where cricket, tennis, and other sports were advertised. He also donated a bottle of fine Scotch whisky as a prize at the black-smiths' annual picnic. Anderson also improved the building with an addition built onto the back in 1910. He gained the respect of his regular customers, who came to know him as a stern yet fair man.

Anderson died quite suddenly in October 1911. There was a huge turnout for his funeral, where his widow, their daughter, and a large contingent of friends, many from the saloon, came to pay their final respects.

The days were numbered for the Regent Saloon. Indeed, all saloon owners were warned that stand-alone saloon licences would not be issued after 1913. Joe Holler and his partner Otto Nitze operated the Regent Saloon during its last months in existence, dodging airborne beer bottles and flying fists.

LELAND HOUSE
1889–1917

Experienced hotelier John McCartney arrived in Victoria from Yale, BC, in 1885 to run the St. Nicholas Hotel on Government Street. In 1888 McCartney also purchased the Snug Tavern on the corner of Queens Avenue and Douglas Street. The Snug Tavern had been in business since the early 1870s, but closed when the last proprietor, John Clemens, died in 1885. Try as he might, McCartney could not obtain a liquor licence for the Snug Tavern. After its third refusal, the licensing board told McCartney that if he built a hotel on that location, he would most likely receive a licence. McCartney then attempted to transfer the licence from the St. Nicholas Hotel to the Snug Tavern, but that application was also refused.

The persistent McCartney built and opened his large two-storey Leland House in September 1889 on a 50-by-100-foot lot on the southeast corner of (213) 2219 Douglas Street and Queens Avenue previously occupied by the Snug Tavern. The Leland House had a bar, a banquet room, a restaurant, six rooms on the main floor, and eight rooms on the second floor. McCartney's application for a liquor licence was finally granted.

McCartney wasn't in business long before he decided to move to the Cariboo. He sold the Leland House to Harry J. Cole in 1891. As the proprietor of the Greyhound Hotel on Water Street in Vancouver, Cole had earned a reputation as a first-rate hotelman. Although the Leland House was relatively new, Cole completely refurbished it and made it his own. Cole spent a considerable sum of money advertising his new hotel and connecting with local clubs and societies. His efforts paid off as a number of clubs rented the Leland House ballroom. The Musical Cork Club, whose members were local singers, was one of the groups that held a social and banquet at the Leland. Member George Thompson sang "Tea Leaves and Snowballs" to an appreciative audience, and proprietor Cole was praised not only for his excellent skill in catering the event, but also for his surprisingly fine rendition of "Kathleen."[54] Cole liked to race horses and was considered quite a philanthropist; he enjoyed giving to worthwhile causes, such as his donation of six bottles of port and sherry to the Jubilee Hospital Directors Banquet.

But it wasn't all wine and roses during Cole's tenure as owner of the Leland House. The Leland was the victim of a break-in when thieves bored holes into the outside barroom door with an auger and stole a number of items from inside the bar. Ng Ah Dick and Yung Bow were charged with robbery when they were tracked down to a house in Chinatown.[55] On another matter, Cole came to the defence of his cook, Lia Boo, who was charged with uttering threats at and using abusive language with a tax collector named Carter. In spite of Cole's testimony, Boo was sentenced to a month in jail for his outburst.[56]

In June 1896 Harry Cole sold the Leland House to Alexander Simpson and his business partner, George Bassett. Cole became manager of the Commercial Hotel at the corner of Douglas and Cormorant Streets.

Alexander Simpson was born in Kirkden, County Angus, Scotland, in about 1854. In 1887 Simpson, along with his wife Mary, son Hugh, and daughter Hannah, immigrated to Canada and then made their way to Victoria. Simpson was a general labourer and eventually began working as a fireman at the Victoria Gasworks.[57] Alexander and Mary Simpson would eventually go on to manage other hotels in Greater Victoria—Alexander at the Rock Bay Hotel from 1895 to 1897, the Blue Post Saloon in 1902, and the Halfway House in Esquimalt from 1905 to 1910; and Mary at the Coach and Horses Hotel in Esquimalt in 1908.

In September 1903 George and Hannah Stokes became the proprietors of the Leland House. Hannah was the daughter of Alexander and Mary Simpson, the previous proprietors of the hotel. George and Hannah were married in a lovely ceremony in Esquimalt on February 2, 1903.[58] George ran the Leland House until December 1905, when he sold to Alexander Hesson. George and Hannah went to the New Inn Hotel in Esquimalt and then to the Ship Inn Hotel in Esquimalt in 1907. The couple then ran the Princess Saloon on Government Street from 1908 to 1911.

Alexander Roger Hesson became the new proprietor of the Leland House on December 14, 1905. Hesson had been a gold prospector during the Klondike Gold Rush and had owned the Irving Hesson Grocers at Hastings and Main Streets in Vancouver.[59]

By 1909 the Leland House and buildings were again in need of updating and repairs. Hesson felt that the hotel was too small and that the whole building needed to be replaced. In the meantime, he applied for a building permit for a property on Bay Street, which was granted on October 27, 1909. His new house was erected beside the Royal Victoria Armoury on Bay Street, just across the street from what would soon be the new home of the Leland House.

In 1912 the magnificent three-storey Andrew Wright Building, containing the Sandringham Apartments, based on the European

The Leland Building, 2515 Douglas Street, replaced
the original Leland House a few blocks to the south.

plan, opened on the northwest corner of 2500–2506 Douglas Street at Bay Street.[60] The Andrew Wright Building was designed by Lord Wilfred Hargreaves (1880–1966), who also designed Lim Bang's Prince George Hotel (see Chapter Five), which became the Douglas Hotel in 1918 and is now known as the Rialto Hotel. Hargreaves also designed the Scott Building just down the street from the Leland, on the southeast corner of Douglas and Hillside Streets (occupied by the Bank of Nova Scotia at the time of writing); the Douglas Building in James Bay; and the Yen Wu Society Building in Chinatown. Like the Dalton Hotel (the former Dominion Hotel) on Yates Street, the Leland Building has an inner courtyard that allowed natural light into the back apartments.[61]

Hesson applied to the Commissioner of Licenses on November 15, 1913, to move his liquor licence to the new Wright Building. His application received ardent opposition from the Voters League and prohibition advocate groups. One argument was that the licensed hotel and apartments would be too close to the North Ward School. Their concerns were dismissed, and in December 1913 Hesson was granted a licence.[62] Two years after his initial application for a transfer of his liquor licence, Hesson moved into the Wright Block. The spacious hotel bar was on the main floor, with hotel rooms and apartments on the upper floors. The new name became the Leland. The original building that John McCartney built in 1885 was demolished by the city to widen Douglas Street.

The Leland House and its bar were short-lived, as Prohibition closed the bar in October 1917 and the hotel was converted into the Leland Apartments in 1918.

Riding high with optimism fuelled by the Klondike Gold Rush, a growing tourist industry, and the completion of the E&N railroad, Victoria's future looked very bright indeed. Victorians were about to reap the benefits of the greatest building boom in the history of the city. By 1905 the first automobile would arrive in Victoria and a whole new industry would energize the economy.

The saloon and hotel bar business was never better, and there was no solid reason to believe it would go sour. But as we will see in the next chapter, increasing opposition to the multitude of drinking establishments in town and the rise of the temperance movement became a real threat to the existence of the saloon. Attitudes were changing, and those who preached temperance were becoming better organized. As early as the 1880s, there were signs of change in the public's tolerance of the saloon and drinking in general.

On March 9, 1899, seven saloon owners were told that if they did not replace their ramshackle wooden buildings with either brick or stone, they would lose their liquor licences. While this move was more for safety than to attack the saloon business, it signalled a change in attitude that saloon owners could no longer expect business as usual. The saloons were already required to close on Sundays, and it was becoming more difficult to obtain and transfer a liquor licence. These restrictions foreshadowed worse things to come. For saloon owners, bartenders, and their customers, the party was about to come to an end. The hotel bars would face the same fate three years later.

CHAPTER FIVE

RESTRICTION TO PROHIBITION

1900-17

It takes a good deal of physical courage to ride a horse. This however I have. I get it at about forty cents a flask, and take it as required.

—Stephen Leacock (1869–1944)[1]

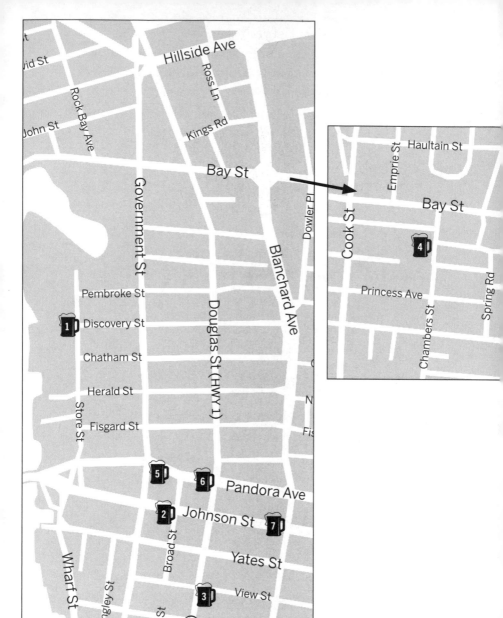

1. Western Hotel
2. Canada Hotel Bar and Grill
3. Balmoral Hotel
4. Lion Brewery Tap Saloon
5. Westholme Hotel
6. Prince George Hotel
7. Kaiserhof to Blanshard Hotel

U ntil 1900, saloons and hotel bars pretty much operated with impunity in Victoria. The freewheeling saloon was open for business twenty-four hours a day, seven days a week. "In British Columbia, where liquor consumption was nearly double the national average in the 1890s, saloons never shut their doors."[2] There were few rules or restrictions, and liquor licences were fairly easy to obtain. However, in the few years that followed, voices opposed to the saloons' stranglehold on the community began to get louder, and to make things worse for the saloon owners, these voices began to gain political clout. By 1910 the tug of war between the temperance movement and those who believed liquor should be unrestricted was intensifying, and the temperance forces were winning.

As long as there had been saloons, there had been those who opposed them. Organized temperance and prohibition forces were active in Victoria as early as 1859, when the American Sons of Temperance, founded in New York in 1842, opened a chapter in Victoria. The Methodists followed that same year on the heels of the Fraser River Gold Rush. "With the coming of the Methodists, a more vigorous and sustained temperance effort was possible."[3] These were but the seeds of temperance and prohibition planted in the community that would take almost sixty years to grow and mature before resulting in a major prohibition victory on October 1, 1917.

The first restrictions on saloon owners came in March 1853 when Governor Douglas passed legislation to license the wholesale and retail sale of liquor in the colony. The following year saw legislation banning Aboriginal people from buying, possessing, and consuming intoxicating beverages.[4] By 1864 the power to grant licences to saloons was transferred to the Board of Justice in Victoria. In 1871 British Columbia became a part of Canada, and "Section 92 of the British North America Act gave the provinces the power to license taverns and saloons in order to raise revenue."[5] And by 1878 the Scott Act was enacted; it was essentially a temperance law that allowed cities and counties to hold a vote in their jurisdiction to decide whether they wished to allow or prohibit the sale of liquor. But even as late as 1909, British Columbia did not have a local option law.[6]

These temperance laws in disguise did not gain much support out in the wild west of Victoria, where most citizens continued to consume copious amounts of intoxicating liquors. The cry to abstain from liquor was never really heard in the city, as it was drowned out by the shouts of joy and bravado emanating from the hundreds of saloons and hotel bars.

In the late 1880s Victoria tried to pass the Sunday blue laws that forbade saloons to open on the Sabbath. These laws were challenged and in most cases were struck down. In 1887 the Habitual Drunkards Act allowed wives and their children, usually the victims of husbands or fathers who were heavy drinkers, to petition to have the men's property rights turned over to a court-appointed trustee. Gambling was outlawed (though the law was mostly ignored), and liquor licence fees were raised for retail outlets.[7]

In 1900 retail outlets selling liquor had their hours of operation restricted. Gone were the days of the wide-open saloon. On the other side of the country on Prince Edward Island, the majority of voters were in favour of prohibition. The island province would remain dry until 1948. Meanwhile in Victoria, a number of events affected the saloon business.

A succession of vicious fires swept through town in 1904, 1907, and 1910, destroying many businesses, including some saloons and hotels. The Driard Hotel, at one time the greatest hotel in Victoria, closed its doors after the Five Sisters fire of 1910 damaged the hotel. In 1905 Great Britain removed one thousand personnel and her naval ships from Esquimalt Harbour and handed the naval base over to the Dominion of Canada, eliminating the $700,000 in revenue that the navy base had generated each year. On May 6, 1906, a small Canadian garrison took over, and the British sailors departed on May 17.[8]

In 1909 there were 109 saloons and hotel bars in Victoria. The Saloon Act of 1911 was the single most devastating piece of legislation to affect the saloon business in British Columbia. Furthermore, changes to the Liquor Act allowed municipalities to close all saloons if they chose to do so. Saloon owners in Victoria were given notice that unless they had a minimum of twenty rooms to their saloons and reapplied for a hotel licence by December 1913, they would be shut down. This action was a thinly veiled effort to limit the number of drinking establishments, since the capital costs of switching over to a hotel were high.[9] Two years later the provincial government supported some form of prohibition. The government insisted that saloon owners had to provide thirty rooms for overnight accommodation.

The Saloon Act effectively ended the reign of the saloon in Victoria and in the rest of British Columbia.

Many saloon owners, like those of the Brown Jug, scrambled to find room to add a hotel or to find a suitable new location to continue their business as a hotel with an attached saloon. In December 1913 H.H. Maloney of the Brown Jug paid $25,000 to purchase the Galpin Block (1884), where he added a buffet dining room and fitted two floors with thirty guest rooms. Because he complied with the new law, Maloney was permitted to keep the Brown Jug Saloon, located next door, in business.[10]

In September 1916 the Liberals won the British Columbia election. The new premier, Harlan Carey Brewster, supported prohibition, and in the subsequent plebiscite on the issue, 36,490 voted in favour of prohibition, with 27,217 opposed.[11] Prohibition took effect on October 1, 1917.

The results of the plebiscite were devastating to the hotels, the brewing industry, and anyone who earned a living either directly or indirectly from the retail and wholesale of liquor. "There was an estimated 3,500 people, with at least 6,000 dependants, directly employed in the saloon and brewing industry. The sudden closing of the bars, saloons and liquor outlets would impose tremendous hardships on those workers."[12] New hotels, like the Brown Jug Inn, spent huge sums of money converting from saloon to hotel in order to comply with the act, only to see their businesses close less than four years later. But not all bars closed, nor did all hotels go broke. Some hotels kept their bars open, selling a product called "near beer" and similar beverages that contained 2.5 percent alcohol.

This chapter will look at a selection of hotels and their bars from 1900 to 1917 and how they fared as ever-tightening restrictions eventually resulted in total prohibition.

WESTERN HOTEL
1885–1925

The Western Hotel was opened by Thomas Shaw in March 1885 on the southwest corner of Store and Discovery Streets. The Western could accommodate up to fifty guests, and it offered a commanding view of the inner harbour to the west, Rock Bay to the north, and the Albion Iron Works to the east. The hotel was located in a quiet area of the city, yet it was close to Spratt's Wharf, the bridge to Rock Bay, and points north by way of the Point Ellice Bridge. The heart of Victoria was but a mere five-minute buggy ride away.

Victoria was fast becoming a desired tourist destination, and to better accommodate the influx of visitors to the city, it became practical to construct an elaborate hotel on a grand scale. In 1885 the leading hotel in Victoria was the Driard. The owners of the Western Hotel planned to build the biggest and best hotel in Victoria. But try as they might, they could not raise the money required for such an ambitious undertaking, and the actual building was scaled back considerably.

The proprietor of the Western Hotel, Thomas Shaw, was energetic and resourceful. He ran for Victoria city council in January 1886, winning as the representative for the Johnson Street Ward. A boilermaker by trade, Shaw also became the head

Sketch of the proposed New Western Hotel, southwest
corner of Discovery and Store Streets, 1891.
VICTORIA ILLUSTRATED

boilermaker and foreman at the Albion Iron Works, located a block east of the Western Hotel.

In the early morning of July 8, 1888, an explosion ripped through the Albion Iron Works. An emery wheel had burst, sending scorching iron fragments high into the air; they acted like missiles, landing in all directions, some as far as a mile away. One of these molten missiles crashed through a second-storey window of one of the rooms at the Western Hotel, passing through two walls before landing on the bed of a third room. The startled guest narrowly escaped death or serious injury, as he had risen out of that bed only a few minutes earlier.[13] That was not the only excitement at the Western Hotel that month. On July 27 the police were called to the hotel when an ex-employee named John had a dispute with a current employee, Miss Henskie. A nasty argument broke out, resulting in John kicking Miss Henskie in the abdomen. He was quickly subdued and arrested, and subsequently charged with and convicted of aggravated assault.

In 1889 William Henry Shewan purchased the Western Hotel for $3,000. The hotel was given a thorough cleaning and received a new coat of paint inside and out, and the rooms were refurbished. Meanwhile, the bar did a roaring business with Joseph Cartedge as bartender. There were no significant problems or incidents reported until the fall of 1903.

Neil Hansen, proprietor of the Western Hotel in 1903, ran a respectable house for the owner, C.J.V. Spratt. On September 16 the head bartender, Peter Nelson, was busy closing the bar for the evening when he was suddenly confronted by two masked men. One of the men stuck a loaded pistol in Nelson's face and demanded the contents of the cashbox as well as his personal valuables.

Nelson quickly complied, and the men made a hasty get-away with twenty-five dollars and Nelson's gold watch. The bartender immediately called the police and provided them with a thorough description of the thieves. The following day, the culprits were apprehended in New Westminster. Suspects Leonard and Lorenzo were held in jail until Detective Palmer of the Victoria Police departed for the mainland to bring the pair back to Victoria to stand trial. They plead guilty and were sentenced to six years in the penitentiary. They were also flogged for the crime.[14]

The Western Hotel was demolished in April 1904 and replaced with the New Western Hotel. This version was much larger and more luxurious. The building contract went to James Auld and was supervised by the manager of the hotel, Neil Hansen. It was announced in the *Victoria Daily Times* on April 17, 1904, that "the new building will be up to date in every particular and rather larger than the old one."[15] Three years later a disaster would threaten to raze the new hotel.

On July 23, 1907, a fire broke out in a small building near Store and Pembroke Streets. Fanned by gusty winds, the fire grew quickly and spread throughout the area. By the time the fire was extinguished, seventy-five buildings had been destroyed over a five-block radius.[16] The cost of the damage was estimated to be well over $200,000. Many of the buildings destroyed were residential houses built entirely of wood. The New Western Hotel survived the fire, but the buildings across the street were not as fortunate, as not one was left standing. A few saloons and a large number of cribs—places where prostitutes and their customers did their business—were also destroyed.

The Shaw Family, ca. 1900. Thomas Shaw, fourth from left,
was the first proprietor of the Western Hotel.
PHOTOGRAPH COURTESY OF CAROL BEST

In 1911 Thomas H. Boyle purchased the New Western Hotel. He advertised, "The New Western Hotel, best twenty cent meal in town. Special rates for room and board, try it."[17] Unfortunately, Mr. Boyle did not own the hotel for long; he succumbed to a fatal seizure in October 1913.

By July 1916 the New Western Hotel had fallen on hard times. On July 12 notice was given in the local newspaper about an auction sale: "Under and by the virtue of a Landlord's Distress Warrant, I have distrained [*sic*] the goods and chattels in and upon the premises known as the Western Hotel, 1930 Store Street . . . contents of 32 bedrooms, dining-room, bar, kitchen, etc. and will offer the same for sale at Public Auction next Friday, July 14 at 10:30 am; Terms for cash sale."[18]

The hotel took another hit when Prohibition ended the sale and distribution of liquor as of October 1, 1917. The New Western Hotel bar remained open, but was permitted to sell only a product nicknamed "near beer." What authorities didn't know was that the owners were secretly selling whisky illegally in the bar; the practice continued for a number of years until they were caught.

Arthur Strom, the proprietor of the hotel from 1920 to 1921, was well known to the authorities. Strom had been in and out of court on a number of occasions, sometimes as the plaintiff, but most often as the defendant. On October 23, 1920, Strom and bartender Thomas Dalton were charged with selling whisky illegally in their hotel bar and fined $300 each. "Magistrate Jay commented strongly upon the recent notoriety attaching to the hotel. He pointed out that Strom had been several times in court recently . . . and said there was no doubt that if the place were under the restraints of the old licensing system, the hotel's license would have been surrendered long ago."[19] Meanwhile, the once elegant hotel had become a rundown rooming house, a haven for prostitutes to ply their trade. It never recovered from the effects of Prohibition, which cut off a significant portion of the hotel's revenue. Like a tree without water, the place began to wither and gradually die. In the Victoria city directory for 1925 there was no longer a reference to the New Western Hotel. By the following year the building that had once housed the hotel was occupied by a different business and had ceased to be a rooming house.

CANADA HOTEL BAR AND GRILL
1892–1917

In the 1850s Simeon Duck purchased lots 159 and 160 along the west side of Broad Street from the corner of Johnson Street; the lots contained a number of small wooden buildings, including a no-name saloon. He commissioned architect William Tuff Whiteway to design the Duck's Building. The result was a handsome three-storey building incorporating a "picturesque eclectic mix of details," from rusticated masonry piers on the ground floor to designer brick and stone lintels, arches, and corbelled cornices on the upper floors.[20] Though it didn't have a name for the first few years, the Canada Hotel Bar and Grill opened in the Duck's Building on the southwest corner of 615 Johnson Street and (62) 1314–1322 Broad Street in 1892.

Simeon Duck was attracted to Victoria due to the gold rush of 1858. After spending time searching for gold in the Cariboo,

Simeon Duck, proprietor of the Canada Hotel, 1314–1322 Broad Street, 1892–96.
IMAGE #G-08561 COURTESY OF THE ROYAL BC MUSEUM AND ARCHIVES

Duck returned to Victoria to open a carriage works business. Initially business was slow until the Cariboo Road was completed, which resulted in a huge demand for carts and carriages. Duck also took a keen interest in public affairs and had an aptitude for politics. His friends urged him to run for office, which he did. After numerous attempts as a candidate, Duck was successful in the provincial election of 1882, and he gradually worked his way up to the position of minister of finance.[21]

A mason by trade, Duck was a member of the Ancient Order of United Workmen until he retired from the trade in 1881.

He was also fascinated by spiritualism, regularly holding séances in his home.[22]

Michael Costin Brown, late of the Adelphi Saloon, was the first proprietor of the unnamed bar inside Duck's new building. Brown operated the bar for the first two years, 1892–93, and added a separate billiards room. Duck took over from Brown in 1894 and found a name for the establishment—the Canada Hotel Bar and Grill. The Duck's Building now housed the Canada Hotel Bar and Grill, Simeon Duck's Carriage Company, and the Knights of Pythias. Most men were attracted to the Duck's Building for what couldn't be advertised in the directory: the brothel located on the upper floors.

Victoria was a hotbed for prostitution, and Broad Street saw more than its fair share of activity. Simeon Duck had considerable influence in the community, and his discreet brothel was ignored by the police and thereby spared from police raids.

> The highest quality houses were around Broughton and Courtney Streets. They catered to society's upper crust, such as members of the nearby Union Club, and were not raided by the police. The bulk of the sex trade though was conducted further north. Herald, Chatham and Fisgard Streets were the heart of the red light district, with some brothels also on Broad and Johnson. Here the sailors, workmen and others further down the social scale could be entertained. Business boomed in the nineteenth century. Even in 1891 there were far more men than women in Victoria, and something of the frontier prevailed.[23]

The police blotter of the 1890s contained numerous arrests for prostitution, and the numbers only increased after Prohibition. Hotels, having been denied revenue from their bars, either closed or sold the unpopular near beer. Prostitutes helped satisfy the appetite of a segment of the public and attracted customers to the hotels. Prostitutes advertised under various euphemisms, such as "dressmakers" or "actresses," but most people knew where to find them. The Duck's Building housed a large brothel for years, and business was very good. "A three-storey red-brick building occupies much of the 1300 block of Broad Street. A chiselled inscription high over the main entrance reads: 'Duck's Building, AD 1892.' The finance minister had replaced a wood building housing his brothel with this still handsome structure, home over the years to a succession of brothels."[24]

Besides finding a hooker, one could also play snooker at the Canada Hotel. The hotel supported all sorts of options for recreation, such as hosting championship billiard tournaments. A three-day tournament took place in November 1907 to determine the city champion. The following year, a large forty-by-sixty-foot gymnasium was built on the second floor. Operated by the Pacific Athletic Club, the gym offered a variety of sporting activities, but specialized in amateur and professional boxing. The club also attempted to bring professional boxing back to town.[25]

In 1909 John Temple, an avid sportsman and the new proprietor of the Canada Hotel, went grouse hunting in Goldstream. He sent five fine fat grouse down to the hotel kitchen to be cooked up for his friends and loyal regulars in the hotel bar to enjoy. Temple, along with head bartender Fred L. Smith, ran a busy bar. Along with the regular patrons, the bar attracted customers from the

Inside the bar at the Canada Hotel Bar and Grill, ca. 1905.
IMAGE #F-02562 COURTESY OF THE ROYAL BC MUSEUM AND ARCHIVES

gymnasium and from the YMCA down the street. On occasion Temple would run afoul of the law, and he was charged with a host of minor infractions of the liquor laws, such as selling liquor to a minor, for which he was fined twenty-five dollars, and selling liquor after hours. But these minor incidents did not dampen his spirits or his enjoyment of working the bar.

In October 1917 Prohibition became law. The bar at the Canada Hotel remained open, legally selling near beer, which contained a very low percentage of alcohol, but like many other establishments that continued on, the Canada Hotel also had secret stashes of whisky and beer discreetly hidden away. In 1919 five bottles of whisky were found and confiscated from the Canada Hotel bar by Sergeant Bolton of the Victoria Police.[26] The bar's reputation was getting so bad that it, along with two other hotel bars in town, was off limits to military personnel.

It didn't help the image of the Canada bar when one of its bartenders, William Bonallo, was arrested for assaulting a woman. It appears that Bonallo knew Emily Johnson when she arrived at the Canada bar to meet a friend one evening. The friend didn't show up, so she and Bonallo chatted into the night, and Bonallo walked Johnson to her residence at the King Edward Hotel. Once in the room, an argument ensued over some money missing from Ms. Johnson's purse. She testified that Bonallo slapped her and continued to physically abuse her. Bonallo denied the charges. Before passing sentence, Magistrate Jay pointed out the bad reputation of the Canada Hotel Bar. He found the defendant guilty and ordered him to pay a $100 fine.[27]

The post-Prohibition party of drinking hidden booze in hotel bars did not continue for long as police enforcement tightened and the courts hit violators in their most vulnerable place—their pocketbooks. The Canada Hotel Bar soon closed, followed by most of the hotel bars in town as their liquor supply dried up.

Simeon Duck died in 1905, and the Canada Hotel became the Nesbitt Hotel in 1919. It eventually closed too, but the building that bears Duck's name survives to this day with a fading ghost sign advertising the Hotel Canada Bar and Grill painted on its brick wall.

BALMORAL HOTEL
1892–1942

Around the same time that the Duck's Building was going up on Broad Street, the Balmoral Hotel building was under construction. The massive three-storey building at (59–61) 1107 Douglas Street, named the Kirk Block, took up an entire block on the east side of the street between Fort and View; the hotel shared frontage onto Douglas Street with other businesses. The hotel was 323 feet long on Douglas Street, 60 feet long on Fort Street, and 60 feet long on View Street. Frederick (Fred) W. Garland, owner and proprietor, opened the Balmoral Hotel on June 1, 1892, to a curious public.

The impressive three-storey, fifty-room, red-brick hotel was made possible due to years of hard work by Fred Garland. He and his wife were joint stewards at the Royal Hospital (the name was later changed to the Royal Jubilee Hospital) in the late 1880s. In 1890 Fred Garland returned to his job as waiter at the New

Douglas Street from Fort Street, Victoria, B.

The Balmoral Hotel, 1107–1109 Douglas Street in the Kirk Block, ca. 1910.

England Bakery at (94) North Park Road. He worked there until May 1891 when he opened the Balmoral Restaurant and Ice-Cream Parlour at (40) Broad Street next to the YMCA, just down the street from the Duck's Building.

The Garlands worked very hard at making their new business a success. Fred advertised the business daily in the newspaper with "Meals at all hours" and "Ice Cream delivered to any part of the city."[28] Their efforts paid off as the restaurant and ice cream parlour proved to be a big hit with the public. Business was so good that, within a year, they needed larger premises. In 1892 Fred Garland had the Balmoral Building constructed at the corner of Douglas and View Streets. While Mrs. Garland went to manage the Poodle Dog Restaurant, Mr. Garland moved the Balmoral Restaurant into his brand new hotel.

The Balmoral Hotel offered the public a spacious dining room lighted by eight large chandeliers, which were illuminated by a combination of electricity and gas. The room had sixteen tables that could comfortably accommodate eighty people; four smaller private rooms were available for quiet meals. The adjoining kitchen contained state-of-the-art ranges and culinary supplies. The well-lit rooms were furnished with finely carved oak and heated by steam. Guests could choose between the less expensive European plan, in which one shared a common bathroom, or the American plan, which included a private bathroom. The massive lobby had a grand piano in one corner, and a corridor led to separate smoking and reading rooms. There was an attractive ladies' parlour and, of course, a bar located at street level.[29]

The other businesses that leased space in the Kirk Block included the Royal Saloon on the Fort Street corner; George

Crowther, engraver; George C. Shaw, manufacturer; John Johnson, bookseller; and the Bodega Saloon on the View Street corner.[30] Although the Balmoral Hotel was sandwiched between two saloons, each occupying a corner of the block, this did not appear to hurt business inside the Balmoral Hotel bar. The Balmoral bar was refurbished in 1898, and the seasoned Alfred Kendall was hired as head bartender. Kendall previously ran the Germania Saloon and was bartender at the Bank Exchange Saloon on Yates Street. The following year he became the proprietor of the Royal Saloon next door to the Balmoral bar.[31]

The early days at the Balmoral Hotel were certainly interesting; from weddings to séances to a foot doctor removing corns for a slight fee, the Balmoral hosted a wide range of attractions. Then there were the unfortunate incidents, like when a guest named Mr. Robert Williams, age seventy-five, who hadn't been seen in days, was found dead in his room by Mr. Garland.[32] In the case of Ah Chick, a Chinese man working in the hotel who was suspected of stealing money from hotel guests' coats, police detectives set up a sting in which they planted marked coins in a coat and waited. Sure enough, the money went missing and the police found the marked coins in Ah Chick's pocket.[33]

In 1896 Fred Garland leased the Balmoral Hotel to Mrs. F.B. Williams, who started renting out a number of the rooms in the Balmoral on a monthly basis. Garland went on to operate the Imperial Cafe. The following year, Mr. and Mrs. Garland moved to Kaslo, BC, where they ran a restaurant until they returned to Victoria some years later to operate the Delhi Cafe on Yates Street.

In 1903 Mrs. Margaret J.G. White became the proprietor of the Balmoral Hotel. This amazing woman had extensive experience in the hospitality industry, having operated four hotels and one saloon. She began her long career as a hotel proprietor at the Brunswick Hotel, which she ran from 1896 to 1909. Along the way Mrs. White added the Dawson Hotel in 1899; the Victoria Theatre on Douglas Street, which became the Imperial Hotel, from 1899 to 1901; and the Bodega Saloon from 1901 to 1909. Lastly she managed the Balmoral Hotel from 1896 to 1903, then owned the hotel until 1912. Margaret White knew how to manage a hotel and how to run a good bar.

The North Coast Land Company purchased the Balmoral Building in 1909 for $100,000. The Balmoral Hotel bar was initially quite small, but it did a very good business despite its size and the presence of two competing saloons on the same block. That all changed in 1911 when the Balmoral Hotel went through an expansion; the alterations included enlarging the bar at the cost of $10,000. The Bodega Saloon was also bought out. The transfer of the licence for the Bodega Saloon to the Balmoral and the conversion of the licence from a saloon licence to a hotel licence were approved in 1912.[34] The larger bar was more popular than ever. Beer sales were exceptional, as shown in the following receipts from the Silver Springs Brewery beer deliveries: "May 1, 1911, six dozen pints of lager; May 2, 1911, twenty-one pints—a mix of stout and ales; May 21, 1911, another twenty-one dozen pints of lager and ales were received."[35]

According to Harry Gregson in his book on the history of Victoria, the outspoken suffragette and champion of women's rights Sylvia Pankhurst walked into the Balmoral Hotel bar one day and demanded to be served. She was refused service, and the matter went to the Supreme Court of British Columbia, which ruled in her favour. The question, which is quite absurd today, was, is a woman deemed "a person" under the liquor legislation? Before women won the right to vote in April 1917, Ms. Pankhurst won the right for all women to legally enter and enjoy a drink in any hotel bar in town.[36]

In 1912 the Balmoral Hotel was sold for $500,000, an enormous amount of money at the time. The German Canadian Trust Company bought the hotel plus other buildings and real estate in Victoria, acquisitions totalling over $1 million.[37] This was a time when the building boom was at its zenith (1910–12), just prior to the worldwide depression that followed in 1913–14. Frank M. Gray was the proprietor of the Balmoral Hotel through the Great War, 1914–18.

The arrival of Prohibition in October 1917 closed the Balmoral Hotel bar, and the following month the hotel went up for sale. Fortunately, the hotel owners found a buyer quickly. The new proprietor, Mr. A. Belanger, refurbished the hotel. The Balmoral Hotel would continue to operate until it was converted into the Balmoral Service Women's Centre in 1942.

LION BREWERY TAP SALOON
1894–1912

The Lion Brewery Tap (or Lyon) Saloon began in 1862, when G.J. Stuart opened the bar on the northwest corner of (116) 2302 Chambers Street and Queens Avenue in Spring Ridge (later renamed the Fernwood District). Victorians had relied

The Lion Brewery Tap Saloon in 1902, with owner Tommy Potter sitting third from the left.
PHOTOGRAPH COURTESY OF GERRY MOORE

on the fresh water found at Spring Ridge to supply their needs since 1843, so it made good sense to the proprietor of the Lion Brewery Tap Saloon to tap into that water supply to brew his own beer.[38] Our look at the Lion Brewery Tap Saloon, however, begins in 1894, when Thomas (Tommy) Potter became the owner. Potter purchased the saloon from the estate of the late George Fairbrother, who had operated the Lion Saloon from 1882 until his untimely death.[39]

Potter was born in the small village of Dunsby, Lincolnshire, England, on December 21, 1824. After years spent as an adventurer and jack of all trades, Potter learned about the California Gold Rush of 1849 and eventually booked passage to San Francisco, arriving there in 1853. The California Gold Rush had peaked the year before, but there was still enough gold to be discovered. When that rush finally petered out, the Fraser River Gold Rush began, bringing thousands of fortune seekers to Victoria, including Potter. Potter spent some time in the goldfields of the Fraser River and the Cariboo before returning to Victoria. He purchased a farm in Saanich, which he worked until he bought the Lion Brewery Tap Saloon in 1894 at the age of seventy.[40]

Tommy Potter was an unconventional character. In 1904 at the age of eighty, he had his gravestone carved and set in place on his plot in the Ross Bay Cemetery, naturally with the date of his death left blank. But Potter had many years left in him. He married in 1907 at the age of eighty-three, and he worked his saloon with the energy of a man twenty to thirty years younger.

In 1909 Potter began the routine of applying to renew his liquor licence through the Commissioner of Licenses when he ran into some opposition to his application. The Victoria School Board had requested that the renewal of the licence for the Lion Saloon be refused. The new George Jay School had been built across the street and a few properties down from the saloon, and the school board felt that the saloon was too near the school, despite the fact that the saloon had been there first, since 1862.[41] The licensing board ruled that it could not terminate the licence and that it was unfair to expect the proprietor to relocate, but the problem remained.

In 1911 Potter decided to apply for a building permit to erect a new hotel where his saloon was located. He planned to spend $15,000 on the venture, which would also improve the corner. To Potter's surprise and amazement, the building inspector refused to grant the building permit. Upon further investigation Potter learned that the school board had approached the city council, urging them to refuse Potter a building permit for his planned hotel. "As the license commissioners have no power to do away with the license the school board sought to accomplish its purpose in another manner."[42] The city solicitor, W.J. Taylor, advised city council that it could not legally prevent the erection of the proposed hotel. It looked as though Potter would get his permit and in turn build his hotel. But the school board and its backers were stubbornly opposed to having school children subjected to a saloon. It was suggested that Potter could have his hotel if he agreed to surrender his liquor licence, for which he would be duly compensated.

Attorney Taylor again advised city council against this action, and within a month Taylor learned that his job as city barrister had been abolished. Furthermore, the majority of city councillors voted to expropriate Potter's property, including his saloon and adjoining lots, for the development of a city yard.[43] When residents learned of this, most signed a petition against expropriation, but it was ignored. Accusations flew accusing Mayor Morley of pushing through the yard scheme not only to get rid of Potter's Lion Saloon, which was probably quite accurate, but also to garner votes for the next election.[44]

In October 1911, Potter, sick and tired of the indecisive mayor and council, put in a $500 claim for compensation due to the long delay in any action regarding his hotel and property. On July 10, 1912, Potter won his case and received $500. Around the same time, city council considered contacting the provincial government about enacting legislation that would effectively cancel any liquor licences in the province of premises that were fronting or immediately adjacent to a public school.[45]

Meanwhile, Potter, now $500 richer, still found the energy

to hold a raffle in the saloon in which ticket holder number eighty-eight won a lovely bay mare. Potter had finally had enough, though, and on October 21, 1912, he applied to have his licence transferred to the Ritz Hotel on Fort Street. Even this application met with opposition, this time from the Independent Order of Good Templars, branches 92 and 84. They felt that there were enough liquor licences in the city core and that no more licence transfers should be accepted. Nevertheless, the transfer was granted and Potter closed the Lion Saloon shortly thereafter.

It may have been the end of the Lion Saloon, but not of Mr. Potter. Potter moved out of his residence inside the saloon and purchased a house about a block away in 1913. The following year, as the old saloon sat empty and untouched, Potter was again in the news. In December 1914 Chong Hop, a notorious gambler in Chinatown, was arrested at his residence on Cormorant Street and charged with conducting a gambling house. Arrested along with Chong Hop was the feisty eighty-nine-year-old Tommy Potter, accused of being a frequent player at those gambling sessions.[46]

In an ironic twist of fate, the old Lion Saloon, which had sat vacant since 1913, was given new life when in February 1916 it was readied to be used as, of all things, a Sunday school.[47] Thomas Potter must have been amused. The old pioneer died on January 19, 1917, at the ripe old age of ninety-two. He had outlived all of his childhood friends, two wives, and his beloved saloon, which fortunately he never lived to see torn down. On December 23, 1917, the old Lion Brewery Tap Saloon building was condemned and soon after was demolished. Queens Park is now located where the saloon once stood, and on a quiet day, if you listen very carefully, you just may hear old Thomas Potter and his friends lifting a pint and sharing a laugh at the Lion Brewery Tap Saloon.

WESTHOLME HOTEL
1911–65

On October 26, 1910, a fire broke out in Spencer's Department Store in downtown Victoria. It grew into a destructive inferno that consumed forty businesses within the Five Sisters Block and damaged the Driard Hotel. The owners of the Driard decided to sell the hotel to David Spencer, who began renovations to make the old Driard his new store. The Driard liquor licence was transferred to the Westholme Hotel Company, which also purchased the Driard's remaining liquor and leased the Driard Hotel bar on a temporary four-month basis until the new Westholme Hotel Building was completed.[48]

The Westholme Hotel Building, a magnificent six-storey Edwardian structure designed by H.S. Griffith, was located at 1417–1419 Government Street on the site occupied by Gideon C. Gerow's carriage foundry since 1862. The Westholme Lumber Company, headed up by Sol Cameron, built and owned the building that housed the hotel and Ivel's Drugstore. Thomas Cavin, president of the Westholme Hotel Company, along with J.T. O'Brien, A. Burdick, F. Clark, and Neil Mackay formed the incorporated stock company that leased the Westholme Hotel and building.[49]

The hotel officially opened on June 1, 1911, with one hundred rooms and mahogany furnishings throughout. The new Westholme also featured the Songhees Grill, located in the basement of the hotel, which had a large orchestra for the public's dining and dancing pleasure.

The unparalleled Songhees Grill received a full-page write-up in the *Colonist* on opening day, August 24, 1911, complete with photographs and illustrations. Superlatives describing this magnificent grill cannot be exaggerated. It was by far the largest and handsomest grill in western Canada, covering six thousand square feet and providing seating for six hundred dinner guests. One dined in splendour as light shone down through magnifying crystal sheets of purple inset into the Government Street sidewalk above, as well as from the wrought-iron lanterns that gave off a mellow amber glow.[50]

Mr. W.E. Murray was the manager and caterer of the Songhees Grill. His impressive resumé included the finest kitchens and top hotels in the major cities of New York, Boston, Philadelphia, and Chicago. The head chef, Mr. E.L. Garnier, arrived from the prestigious Union League Club of Chicago. Murray and Garnier chose twelve undercooks and hand-picked thirty-five experienced waiters from hundreds of applicants.[51]

Opening night for the Songhees Grill was a resounding success. Not only was the giant room filled to capacity, but sixty-five groups of diners were reluctantly turned away. The large and elegant room was decorated predominantly in pink, with a fragrant hint of sweet peas adorning the air. Parties from two to ten were among the diners, the ladies looking lovely in their colourful summer evening dresses and the men dressed in black evening suits.[52]

Points of Interest *In and Around*

Victoria THE "Venice of Canada"

With Compliments of

HOTEL WESTHOLME

Victoria's New Hotel, Opened June 1, 1911

The Westholme Hotel brochure. Produced by the Sweeney-McConnell Press, 1911.

Lobby and bus of the Westholme Hotel.

Wonderful music played throughout dinner, with an occasional vocal performance lending to the magic of the evening.

It was only a few months after the gala opening that the Westholme Lumber Company attempted to sell the hotel for $64,000 to Hugh Springer of Vancouver. Springer had plans to expand the hotel by building a 130-room annex on the Pandora side. But the licence was temporarily held by the sheriff, F.G. Richards, as the court-appointed representative ordered to sell the assets of the hotel to pay off debts owed. The legal arguments went on for months before the situation was resolved. Mr. Springer withdrew his bid to purchase the hotel, and the original holder of the licence, Sol Cameron, transferred it to Frank F. Trotter in June 1913. But that wasn't the end of Sheriff Richards's involvement. Trotter would operate the hotel for seventeen months until the sheriff became involved once more.

On October 29, 1914, Sheriff Richards, by virtue of the Landlord's Distress Warrant, took possession of the goods and chattels of the Westholme Hotel for a second time, and an auction was set to sell the hotel and all of the contents therein. Finally, in early 1915, the Westholme Hotel was sold to Mr. K.A. Ray of West Vancouver, who in 1919 formed the K.A. Ray Limited Company.[53] Edward Bonner took over the duties of managing the hotel from Frank Trotter.

Roy Rickman, a new hire, had received his bartender's licence in March 1917, but the arrival of Prohibition on October 1, 1917, closed most hotel bars in town. The Westholme bar continued to sell near beer and other products, but in November 1917 the Westholme bar, along with two other hotel bars in town, was raided, and a large quantity of Devonshire cider was confiscated by Prohibition police. The case went to court, where the defendants claimed that they were authorized to sell the cider during off-hours before Prohibition, so it seemed logical that they could continue to sell the product during regular bar hours now that Prohibition was the law. The provisions of the Prohibition Act allowed for the sale of any beverage as long as it contained no more than 2.5 percent alcohol. Unfortunately, the sweet Devonshire cider contained 3 percent alcohol and therefore was banned under the act. The three bars in question, which included the Westholme Hotel bar, had their cider confiscated and were fined fifty dollars each.[54]

One by one the hotel bars closed, and in most cases the hotels followed. The Westholme was one of a handful of exceptions, managing to keep its doors open until 1965, when it was refitted and reopened as part of the Century Inn.

PRINCE GEORGE HOTEL
1912–17

The industrious Chinese businessman Lim Bang opened the Prince George Hotel on January 24, 1912, at the southwest corner of 1450 Douglas Street and Pandora Avenue. The five-storey Edwardian Commercial–style brick building was designed by Lord Wilfred Hargreaves during the building boom of 1910–13, just prior to the outbreak of the First World War.

Lim Bang was born in Victoria in 1884, where his father, Lim Dat, worked as a general merchant. Lim Bang and his brother

Advertisement for the Prince George Hotel, *British Colonist*.

Lim Yet were part of the first small group of Chinese Canadians admitted to public school, but they were segregated from the rest of the students due to the prejudices of the times. Lim Bang married in 1903 and had four children. The family chose to live outside of Chinatown. Lim Bang had one of the first automobiles in town, which he used to drive to his various businesses, including his own brickworks in Sidney, BC, and later his splendid Prince George Hotel.[55]

Lim Bang hired Jason Graham, from the Victoria Hotel, as manager, Harry Porter to manage the bar, and F.W. Kostenbader (see the Kaiserhof Hotel profile in this chapter) to manage the cafe and catering. In the basement a billiards room and a barber shop were under construction. On the main floor was the spacious lobby, and two good-sized reading rooms and a music room could be found down the corridor. The floors above contained the spacious and airy rooms, each with striking new furnishings.[56] On opening day the hotel filled with guests thanks in part to members of the Federation of Labour, which was holding its annual meeting in Victoria.

For whatever reason, the new hotel did not last long under Lim Bang's ownership. Less than seven months after opening, on

July 12, 1912, the hotel and its contents went up for sale. By virtue of the Landlord's Distress Act, Sheriff Richards held an auction in the rotunda of the Prince George Hotel. After a brief bidding battle, Mr. C.K. Courtney was the winner. He paid $20,000 for the hotel and all of its contents. Shortly after Courtney became the new owner, proprietor Jason Graham stepped down and William L. Coates became the new proprietor.[57] The following month, Courtney set up the Prince George Hotel Corporation.

A number of functions took place in the hotel, including the inaugural meeting of the BC Cricket Association and a large banquet put on by the Orange Lodge of Victoria in celebration of Guy Fawkes Day, with the mayor in attendance. These events and other bookings by organizations and clubs helped sustain the new hotel.

A strange and tragic incident took place in one of the rooms of the hotel in June 1913. Mr. F.A. Arone, an American guest who had been staying at the hotel for a month, was chatting with a few acquaintances in the lobby of the Prince George Hotel when he decided to go purchase a cigar. He wandered into the bar, where he had a glass of beer. Arone declined another beer from the bartender, stating that he was tired and that it was time for him to turn in. He went back into the lobby and took the elevator to his third-floor room. Five minutes later, another guest, Henry Stadthagen, rushed down the stairs and claimed that someone on the third floor had just attempted to rob him at gunpoint. The police were called, and Detectives Murray and Carlow arrived shortly afterward. They were quickly apprised of the situation and found that Arone fit the description of the suspect. While Carlow went outside to keep an eye on the fire escape in case

The Prince George Hotel in the Lim Bang Building, 1912.
COURTESY OF THE CITY OF VICTORIA ARCHIVES, #M06881

the suspect tried to flee that way, Murray and the hotel night clerk went upstairs to Arone's room. Murray knocked on the door, identified himself, and ordered the door unlocked. Arone refused. Murray then had the night clerk open the door with the passkey, and that's when a loud gunshot rang out, followed immediately by a gasp and a thud. Murray pushed the door open and saw Arone on the floor in a pool of blood; he had fatally shot himself in the head.[58]

After Henry Stadthagen was questioned, it became clear that Arone had not tried to rob him after all, but that Stadthagen had startled Arone as he came off the elevator and Arone had pulled out his pistol to protect himself. That's when the frightened Stadthagen ran down the stairs and claimed attempted robbery. It was later learned that the deceased had said that his wife and daughter had been killed in a hurricane in the midwest United States only months earlier.

During the inquest it came to light that Arone had checked into the hotel under a false name, and that his real name was Theodore H. Braker, a recent employee of the Alexander Hotel in San Francisco. But why the deception, and what did Mr. Braker, if that was his real name, have to hide?

It turned out that Theodore H. Braker, alias F.A. Arone, had also worked as a clerk in a hotel in Klamath Falls, Oregon, which he had left in a hurry after stealing a large sum of money from the hotel owners. When he arrived in Victoria and checked into the Prince George Hotel, Braker prepaid his hotel bill for one month, and it was the last day before the following month's rent was due when he killed himself. Only one dollar was found in his pocketbook. Furthermore, Braker had been infatuated with a woman in San Francisco who was visiting Victoria. He had asked for her hand in marriage, but she had refused. The inquest received a letter from the San Francisco Police that contained a photograph confirming that the deceased was indeed Theodore H. Braker and that he was already married.[59]

In 1913–14 there was a worldwide depression that coincided with the end of the mining boom. As of December 1913 stand-alone saloons were no longer being licensed, and this gave hotel bars a bit of a financial boost, as those drinkers had to go somewhere. In August 1914 Joseph William Wallis took over as proprietor of the Prince George Hotel from William Coates just as Great Britain declared war on Germany and Canada quickly followed suit. On New Year's Eve 1914, the Prince George Hotel advertised, "The House of Plenty full-course meals, and celebrations to bring in the New Year, all are welcome, especially all those in military service."[60]

The Prince George Hotel closed just after Prohibition in October 1917. The 1918 city directory listed the old site of the hotel as vacant.[61] Later in 1918 a new owner would reopen the hotel under a new name, the Douglas Hotel, and a new chapter would begin for the old hostelry.

KAISERHOF TO BLANSHARD HOTEL
1912–15

The history of the Kaiserhof Hotel is brief yet interesting. In 1880 John Draut opened the BC Grocery and Bakery on

The Kaiserhof Hotel bar, damaged from the May 1915 riot.
IMAGE #C-07552 COURTESY OF THE ROYAL BC MUSEUM AND ARCHIVES

the southwest corner of 1320–1324 Blanshard and Johnson Streets. In 1891 Draut refitted his store into an unnamed saloon (see the Klondike Hotel Bar profile in Chapter Four). In 1898 the saloon became part of the Klondike Hotel. In 1906 Harry Rudge became the last proprietor of the Klondike Hotel, and in September 1912 Rudge applied to transfer the licence to F.W. Kostenbader.

Max Leiser purchased the Klondike Hotel in June 1912 with plans to demolish the building and replace it with the Kaiserhof Hotel. Max Leiser was persuaded to come to Victoria by his brother Simon Leiser, of Simon Leiser & Company, who had been in Victoria since 1887. On his arrival Max bought half of the business of Urquhart & Pither, wholesale liquor merchants, which then became Pither & Leiser.[62] Max Leiser also invested in property and commercial buildings in town, including the Klondike Hotel.

Leiser hired well-known architect Thomas Hooper to design his new hotel. The years 1909 to 1912 proved to be the most prolific period in Hooper's amazing career, which coincided with the building boom that lasted until 1913.[63] Hooper's unique, bold design stood out at the corner of Blanshard and Johnson Streets. The Edwardian decorative features included cream-glazed terracotta and tan bricks with alternating bands of brick and terracotta on the first floor, resulting in a striking and dramatic exterior.[64] The new building, named the Max Leiser Building after its owner, housed the thirty-six-room Kaiserhof Hotel, managed by Frederick W. Kostenbader.

Kostenbader arrived in Victoria in 1908 from Seattle, where he had been the steward at the Perry and Butler Hotels. He became the steward at the new Empress Hotel and was the head caterer of other local hotels, including the Prince George Hotel (which became the Douglas Hotel in 1918) on Douglas Street.[65] Kostenbader was elected president of the Deutscher Verein (German Club) at its general meeting in February 1911. A very able speaker, he presided over numerous events sponsored by the German Club, such as the celebration of Kaiser Wilhelm II's fifty-third birthday, which took place in the ballroom of the Empress Hotel in January 1912. Max Leiser leased his new hotel to Kostenbader, who received his liquor licence on July 18, 1912.

It wasn't until January 1913 that the Kaiserhof Hotel was ready to open. On January 14 the cafe and bar opened, followed by the hotel rooms. The bar at the Kaiserhof was a reflection of the best *bierpalast*, or German hall, that one could find in Bavaria: "On the ground floor is a large bar and lunch counter furnished handsomely in mission oak and mahogany with all the requisite appurtenances, special attention having been paid to the decorations, those on the walls being frescoes of most artistic design and execution in representation of a typical German tap-room."[66] Rear doors in the bar led outside to a spacious, fenced-in beer garden. Humbser German beer with sausage was favoured over local beer, and more German than English was spoken.

In the spring of 1913 a number of clever advertisements promoting the Kaiserhof Hotel began showing up in the local *Colonist* newspaper: "Sunday's Dinner—Give your wife a rest, have dinner here where everything is best." Or "Good Old Bohemia—The Kaiserhof is one of the best places to enjoy Bohemian life, in fact, it is the *only* place."[67]

Five-cent token used in the Kaiserhof bar, 1912–14.
GLEN A. MOFFORD COLLECTION

The Kaiserhof advertised itself as the "Home of German Hospitality" and was significant for its association with the early German community that added to the varied multicultural makeup of Victoria. Just as the Grand Pacific Hotel on Johnson Street, opened by the Bossi brothers, could be viewed as the quintessential Italian hotel, the Kaiserhof was the classic German establishment.

Large quantities of German capital were flowing into British Columbia, much of it through the hands of Count Konstantin Alvo von Alvensleben, who was said to have connections to the Kaiser.[68] Relations between Great Britain and Germany, at least on the surface, appeared to be very good, but that would all change by the summer of 1914. So, too, did things forever change for the Kaiserhof Hotel.

The fragile peace in Europe kept by a series of alliances broke down when Archduke Franz Ferdinand of Austria was assassinated in July 1914. Tensions escalated until August 4, when Great Britain declared war on Germany; Canada followed Britain's lead the next day. People found themselves swept up by a wave of patriotism, and it was in this atmosphere of xenophobia against anything

Rioters outside the Kaiserhof Hotel, May 1915.
IMAGE #C-02709 COURTESY OF THE ROYAL BC MUSEUM AND ARCHIVES

German that Kostenbader wisely decided to change the name of the Kaiserhof to the Blanshard Hotel. A small advertisement in the *Colonist* announced the name change and the appointment of a new manager, C.T. Marshall, in October 1914.[69] Kostenbader stayed on as the proprietor of the Blanshard Hotel until a major event took place in May 1915 that made his job untenable.

On Saturday morning, May 8, 1915, Victorians received the news that a German submarine had torpedoed and sunk the luxury liner ss *Lusitania* and that all 1,400 passengers and crew had perished. This bitter news was splashed all over the front page of the local paper, in which Victorians also learned that fifteen victims of the attack were from Victoria, including Lieutenant

J. Dunsmuir, the son of the Honourable James Dunsmuir, former premier of British Columbia.

There was already a considerable anti-German sentiment in Victoria due to the outbreak of war between the British and German Empires, but news of the sinking of the *Lusitania* fanned the flames of "anti-Hun" out of control. Outraged citizens began showing up in front of German-owned businesses, including the Blanshard Hotel, the evening following the sinking. A riot broke out in which the exterior and interior of the hotel were damaged before the crowd moved on to the German Club and did as much damage there as they could. Swelled by additional rioters, the mob returned to the Blanshard Hotel, where they sacked and looted the place until the mayor was forced to read the riot act and call for reinforcements from the army based in Esquimalt.

That single event ended Kostenbader's term as the proprietor of the Blanshard Hotel, and all reminders of Germany that weren't destroyed by the rioters were quickly removed. In August 1915 Kostenbader applied to have the licence transferred to Alexander McCool. On September 16, 1915, during a special meeting of the Board of Licensing Commissioners, the transfer was granted. The name of the hotel changed with the new proprietor, becoming the Cecil Hotel.[70]

Frederick Kostenbader, like many ethnic German Canadians, left Canada, most likely returning to Seattle. Max Leiser continued to own the hotel until his death of natural causes in 1935.

There is one footnote to this story worth mentioning. The five-cent token of the Kaiserhof (see illustration on page 227) is from my personal collection. I purchased it about ten years ago from a local Victoria family. Ronald Greene, a Victoria historian with an interest in historic tokens, tracked down the history of the ones from the Kaiserhof Hotel: "In 1920 Messrs. Grant and Wilson became the proprietors of the Cecil Hotel. Charles Wilson had a son named Billy and it is to him that we owe the survival of the Kaiserhof tokens. About 1926 Billy, who attended a small private boys school on Rockland Avenue called the Collegiate School, took bags full of the tokens to school and with his classmates devised a game they called 'Flipping Kaiserhofs.' Several of these 'boys' still had a few of the Kaiserhof tokens forty years later when I tracked them down."[71]

Prohibition was called the "noble experiment" in which society banned the evil influence of alcohol. It was generally believed that once the temptation of abusing spirituous liquors was eradicated, the world would rid itself of most of its problems, such as poverty, immorality, ill health, crime, and insanity. The Prohibition Act became law in 1917, during the First World War. Those not on the front lines in France or Belgium wanted to make their own personal sacrifice to create the sense of doing something important for the war effort.[72]

But in the end, Prohibition caused more problems than it solved. The illicit sale of alcohol on the black market made a fortune for gangsters, while legitimate businesses, such as many of the hotels in Victoria, simply went broke. The "noble experiment" lasted only three years in British Columbia before the majority of voters ended Prohibition in favour of government control.

AN ODE TO JOHN BARLEYCORN

My bar is torn down,
back to the dust from which it came.
The street is changing,
never to be the same.
My glass is near empty,
never to be filled here again.
And the old dance floor is gone,
only the echo of songs still remain.
Goodbye my old friend,
my port in the storm,
this place filled with youthful memories,
its loss few will mourn.
I lift my glass for the last time,
and toast this place where I spent years,
recalling friends who have come and gone,
and too many good beers.

      —Glen A. Mofford

THE BOTTOM OF THE GLASS

Whilst traveling through Afghanistan, we lost our corkscrew. Had to live on food and water for several days.

—W.C. Fields (1880–1946)[1]

The phenomenon known as the saloon lasted only sixty-two years, from 1851 to 1913. The hotel bar existed from 1859 to 1917, with some bars lingering on for a few more years, selling near beer and other products with less than 2.5 percent alcohol.

Prohibition was the single most devastating event to happen to the hotel bars after the saloons closed in 1913. Most of the hotels simply closed as well, but a few had enough business to survive the shuttering of their bars. "In 1917, at the time of Prohibition, many of these hotels had suffered financially and gone broke, but within a few years they opened again under the guise of respectability; in reality they were brothels."[2] It took years for the remaining hotels to recover from the effects of losing their hotel bars, and most just went out of business.

It didn't take long for government to discover that the "noble experiment" of Prohibition did not work. In 1918 the provincial government created the office of Prohibition Commissioner, with W.C. Findlay as the first commissioner. Mr. Findlay was to oversee and coordinate the enforcement of the Prohibition Act. Ironically he was one of the first to be arrested under the act when he was convicted of bootlegging. Findlay was fined $1,000 and sentenced to two years in jail.[3]

Just because the saloons were gone did not mean that people stopped drinking. If someone wanted a drink badly enough they found a way to get it. A series of "blind pigs" opened; the American version was called the "speakeasy." These clubs sold alcohol to anyone who was willing to pay the inflated price. "In a pattern that is all too familiar, artificial scarcity of a popular drug (in this case alcohol), will inevitably lead to higher prices, a black market, and astonishing sums of illicit cash."[4] Bootlegging made Al Capone and many other Americans rich, as rum-running would do for many Canadians during the long dry spell in the United States.

In 1921 the majority of voters in British Columbia rejected Prohibition, instead opting for government control. Each jurisdiction voted on a local option whether to allow beer by the glass. In April 1925 the first beer parlours opened in the areas of the province that had voted for beer by the glass. The majority of voters in Victoria opted against the proposal, resulting in a dry Victoria without beer parlours until 1954.

It wasn't until 1972 that the provincial government, under the New Democratic Party, introduced the neighbourhood pub. This alternative to the hotel beer parlour was based on the pubs in Great Britain where men and women could enjoy a drink together in a smaller establishment, usually within walking distance of their homes. It wasn't a return to the old-style saloon, but it was a return to the stand-alone pub without the requirement of a hotel. But that is a topic best left for a future book.

Saloons and hotel bars played a significant role in the development of early Victoria. Monuments to these exciting times can still be found in the wonderful architecture of the historic brick buildings that were carefully preserved in downtown Victoria. Beautiful buildings that were once luxurious hotels or busy saloons have survived through the years and have found new uses within a modern context.

While the preservation of our historic buildings is essential both aesthetically and to enrich our knowledge of how past generations lived, these edifices can best be appreciated when one knows a bit more about their history. Today's Bay Centre may take on a whole new significance if you knew that it was built on the bones of one of the most prominent hotels of the 1890s—the Driard. The next time you find yourself walking past the tattoo parlour on Wharf Street near Bastion Square, you may want to stop for a moment and admire the place that used to house one of the versions of the Ship Inn Saloon. Or when you find yourself walking over the surviving purple glass in the sidewalk along 1417–1419 Government Street, you might appreciate that you are walking above the old Songhees Grill operated by the owners of the Westholme Hotel a little over a century ago. Fortunately, we can still visit many of the sites where these great old hostelries once existed and follow in the footsteps of these pioneers. Mike Powers, the energetic proprietor of the Garrick's Head, would most likely be pleased to know that his once proud saloon has been resurrected and enlarged and is selling pints of beer like it did one hundred years ago.

The brief era in which saloons and hotel bars were prominent is a fascinating and colourful chapter in the overall history of Victoria. It was a time of rapid change and growth that has enriched our lives today.

TIMELINE OF SIGNIFICANT EVENTS

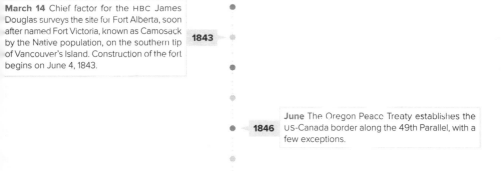

1840

March 14 Chief factor for the HBC James Douglas surveys the site for Fort Alberta, soon after named Fort Victoria, known as Camosack by the Native population, on the southern tip of Vancouver's Island. Construction of the fort begins on June 4, 1843.

1843

June The Oregon Peace Treaty establishes the US-Canada border along the 49th Parallel, with a few exceptions.

1846

January 13 Vancouver Island leased to the Hudson's Bay Company.

1849

The Puget Sound Agricultural Company transfers operations to Vancouver Island.

Richard Blanshard, the first Royal Governor, arrives on Vancouver Island.

1850

May 10 The ship *Tory* arrives from England with the first settlers in Victoria.

1851–1855 J.D. Pemberton surveys the land surrounding Fort Victoria and the first street grid is completed.

1851

June 9 James Yates purchases two lots of land on the west side of Wharf Street where his first house and the first saloon, The Ship Inn, are built.

Hudson's Bay Company chief factor James Douglas is appointed Governor of the Colony of Vancouver Island.

March 27 Governor James Douglas introduces liquor licences to moderate the retail sale and wholesale of liquor and to raise revenue for the tiny settlement.

1853

1854

The first census records 232 residents (half under the age of twenty), 79 houses, and 12 shops.

Parsons Bridge Hotel opens (later known as the Six Mile House).

1857

Charles Bayley opens the first hotel in Victoria, the Bayley's Hotel, on the NE corner of Yates and Government.

April 25 The first of many ships arrive in Victoria with gold seekers to the Fraser River. Within the next six weeks 20,000 persons arrive, prompting a building boom.

The first brick building, appropriately named the Victoria Hotel, is built for George Richardson on the northeast corner of Government and (Rae) Courtney Streets.

Chinatown is established.

1858

The Sons of Temperance, an American prohibition society, opens a chapter in Victoria.

May 30 Vancouver Island becomes a Crown Colony as the HBC lease expires.

1859

January 23 John D. Carroll opens the Brown Jug Saloon on the southeast corner of Fort and Government.

1861–1862 The Cariboo Gold Rush is widely publicized.

1860

January 1 Victoria is declared a "free port" by Sir James Douglas. The first Victoria directory is published (in San Francisco).

July 12 Three retail ale and porter liquor licences are granted for twelve wholesale and twenty-six retail licences are issued.

1861

August 2 The City of Victoria is incorporated, with Thomas Harris as the first mayor (elected by acclamation on August 16). A bill passes forbidding the construction of wooden structures over eighteen feet high, or greater than one storey, within city limits.

1862

September 28 Gas service commences, with the first gas-light lamp illuminated outside Carroll's liquor store on Yates Street.

1862–1864 The old HBC fort is demolished and replaced by the brick buildings of Bastion Square.

1864

Gold is found on the Leech River just north of Victoria.

1865

Esquimalt is officially made the base for the Royal Navy Pacific Fleet.

1865–1870 Economic downturn as the gold rushes end. The economy is sluggish.

1866

November 17 Vancouver Island and the mainland are united into a single Crown Colony called British Columbia, with the capital at New Westminster.

Victoria officially becomes the capital city of the colony of British Columbia.

1868

1870–1871 Economic prosperity returns to Victoria, doubling the population to 5,000.

1870

Victoria now boasts eighty-five licensed drinking establishments, "many of which are in addition to brothels and gambling houses."

1871

August 1 British Columbians vote to join confederation with Canada.

The high-class Driard Hotel is the first to have piped in water from a local well.

1873–1880 Economic downturn. Victoria's population remains static at 6,000 with fifty-six saloons.

1873

September George Richardson, owner of the Victoria Hotel, accidentally causes a gas explosion in his hotel when he enters the parlour with a lighted candle while investigating a foul odour.

1876

November 30 Minors and saloons: Youths under the age of sixteen are not allowed to enter and remain on their premises. There is a $50.00 fine for every offence.

1877

August 2 Death of Sir James Douglas.

The Canadian Temperance Act, also known as the Scott Act, is introduced by Sir Richard William Scott. It provides for an option wherein municipalities can opt in by plebiscite to accept or opt out of the prohibition of alcohol.

1878

1881–1892 Optimism fuelled by railway boom results in prosperity.

1881

The Women's Christian Temperance Movement (WCTU) from the United States begins a chapter in British Columbia.

1882

The first electric powered street lights are erected in the City of Victoria

A large fire destroys many of the buildings between Government, Cormorant (now Pandora Avenue), and Store Streets.

1883

Electricity becomes available.

1884

December 15 Three hotels experience new electric lighting: the Colonial, the Occidental, and the California.

1889

Electric streetcar service begins. First sewers are built.

1890

1891 1891–1892 Local smallpox epidemic hits the Native population especially hard. The Burnes House closes, in part, as a direct result of the epidemic.

January 1 Legislation is passed requiring saloons to close on Sundays (Scott Act of 1885), but loopholes in the law keep Sunday drinking. Hotel competition is fierce—fifty-five are licensed, and a number of unlicensed saloons never close their doors (open twenty-four hours, seven hours a day).

1892

1893 1893–1896 Worldwide recession.

Fixed hours of operation for the saloons are set. They are to be opened no later than midnight Mondays to Fridays and until 11 PM on Saturday nights.

Fort Street is paved with wooden paving blocks.

1896 Victoria & Sidney Railway opens up the peninsula to residential populations.

The drop in seal skin prices due to a glut in the market and other factors affect the revenue of certain hotels and saloons in the city.

1897 Klondike Gold Rush brings some relief to Victoria merchants.

March 9 "Unsuitable Saloons": Seven ramshackle saloons will no longer be granted licence transfers so "that these eyesores may be removed as speedily as possible."

1898 **September 29** National Referendum on Prohibition.

1899–1913: Prosperity returns, resulting in a massive building boom.

1899

1900 Restrictions on business hours are imposed on the saloons. Fifty-five premises are licensed. The city of Vancouver eclipses Victoria in importance.

January 22 Queen Victoria dies.

1901 1900–1910 Tourism is on the rise as travel becomes easier and more sophisticated.

September 4 Mount Baker Hotel in Oak Bay burns down. Fire is the single most destructive natural force in Victoria, with three major fires occurring in 1904, 1907, and 1910.

1902

The first wireless is set up in the Driard Hotel.

January 20 The Empress Hotel opens, monopolizing the "prestige trade" and forcing some hotels to close.

1905 1905–1909 The street numbering system is changed. Confusion continues for years.

The Canadian Opium Act outlaws the manufacture or sale of opium. Six known opium dens close.

The Local Option League is formed, headed by Vancouver businessman E.B. Morgan and made up of WCTU members, evangelical churches, and other temperance groups, with the aim of convincing the government to enact a local option law.

1907 **July 23** A disastrous fire destroys seventy-five structures over a six-block radius, proving to be the worst fire in the city's history to date.

1908

October Fire destroys the Five Sisters Block in downtown Victoria.

1910–1912 Real estate speculation and building boom at its zenith, resulting in a number of new buildings replacing older structures. This transforms the look of downtown. Corner lots in town sell for $15,000. The Balmoral Hotel is sold for $500,000.

1910

1911 The provincial government gives notice to saloon owners that they have three years to convert to hotels, with a minimum of twenty rooms, or face closing.

1913 Pro-prohibition Provincial Liberal Government under Harlan Brewster takes power.

1913–1914 Worldwide depression reduces trade, marking the end of the mining boom.

January 14 Legislation is passed denying liquor licences to stand-alone saloons.

July 1914–November 1918 The Great War.

1914

1915 **May 15** German-owned businesses are looted by angry mobs after news that a German U-boat has sunk the *Lusitanian*. The Kaiserhof Hotel, as well as the German Club, is damaged, resulting in the hotel's sale; it is renamed the Blanshard.

February The army is called to help clear roads from a record snowfall.

1916

April Women receive the right to vote.

October 1 Prohibition of the retail sale of alcohol becomes law. Eighty hotels are directly affected; many soon close or become run down from the lack of liquor revenue.

1917

1917–1933 The Volstead Act passes in the United States, enacting the prohibition of alcohol; widespread bootlegging begins as some Canadians get rich on the proceeds of rum-running to the US after 1921.

1918 Mary Ellen Smith of Vancouver is the first woman to be elected to the Legislature.

1918–1923 Worldwide recession.

1920 **October 20** Prohibition ends in favour of government control of liquor sales and distribution in a plebiscite, with 92,095 votes to 55,448.

1921 **February 23** The Government Liquor Act gives control (to the provincial government) over the sale, distribution, and consumption of alcohol. Restrictions include banning "near beer" and setting the age of legal consumption at twenty-one.

January 1 At 2 AM all traffic switches to the right-hand side of the road from the left.

1922

June 15 The first government liquor stores appear; the first one is on Yates Street.

June 20 Plebiscites on the question of allowing establishments (hotels and clubs) to sell beer by the glass are held across the province, resulting in a close "dry" victory. Local option is adapted, in which those areas that voted for beer by the glass are granted the first liquor licences. Victorians reject beer by the glass.

1924

BIBLIOGRAPHY

Allen, Harold Tuttle. *Forty Years' Journey: The Temperance Movement in British Columbia to 1900*. Victoria: Self-published, 1982.

Anderson, Alexander Caulfield. *British Columbia Directory*. Victoria: R.T. Williams, 1882–83.

Baskerville, Peter A. *Beyond the Island: An Illustrated History of Victoria*. Burlington, ON: Windsor Publications, 1986.

Berton, Pierre. *Klondike: The Last Great Gold Rush, 1896–1899*. Toronto: McClelland & Stewart, 1972.

Campbell, Robert A. *Demon Rum or Easy Money: Government Control of Liquor in British Columbia from Prohibition to Privatization*. Ottawa: Carleton University Press, 1991.

——. *Sit Down and Drink Your Beer: Regulating Vancouver's Beer Parlours, 1925–1954*. Toronto: University of Toronto Press, 2001.

Carr, Emily. *The Book of Small*. Markham, ON: Fitzhenry & Whiteside, 2004.

Clark, Cecil. "Mike Powers Wouldn't Talk." *Islander Magazine*, January 23, 1972.

——. *The Best of Victoria, Yesterday and Today: A Nostalgic 115-Year Pictorial History of Victoria*. Victoria: The Victoria Weekly, 1973.

Colonial Despatches of Vancouver Island and British Columbia, 1846–1871. 9499 305/4, Humanities and Computing Centre, University of Victoria.

Cross, Rosemary James. "Lord Wilfrid Hargreaves." In *Building the West: The Early Architects of British Columbia*, edited by Donald Luxton, 365. Vancouver: Talonbooks, 2007.

Duffus, Maureen, ed. *Beyond the Blue Bridge: Stories from Esquimalt*. Victoria: Desktop Publishing, 1990.

Elmer, Barry, and Dorothy Mindenhall. "Edward McCoskrie, 1822–1893." In *Building the West: The Early Architects of British Columbia*, edited by Donald Luxton, 163. Vancouver: Talonbooks, 2007.

Emberson, Alfred. *Victoria Illustrated*. Victoria: Ellis & Co., 1891.

Fawcett, Edgar. *Some Reminiscences of Old Victoria*. Toronto: William Briggs, 1912.

First Victoria Directory. Victoria: Edward Mallandaine & Co., 1860, 1863, 1869.

Gordon, Elizabeth. "Colourful Simeon Duck." *Islander Magazine*, June 24, 2010. http://victoriahistory.ca/blog/2010/06/colourful-simeon-duck/.

Grant, Peter. *Victoria: A History in Photographs*. Vancouver: Altitude Publishing, 1995.

Green, Valerie. *Upstarts and Outcasts: Victoria's Not-So-Proper Past*. Victoria: TouchWood Editions, 2000.

Greene, Ronald. "The Brown Jug Saloon of Victoria: Token History." *British Columbia History Magazine*, Spring 2008.

———. "Token History: The Kaiserhof Hotel." *British Columbia Historical News*, July 2003.

Gregson, Harry. *A History of Victoria, 1842–1970*. Victoria: Observer Publishing, 1970.

Hamilton, Douglas L. *Sobering Dilemma: A History of Prohibition in British Columbia*. Vancouver: Ronsdale Press, 2004.

Hanna, Christopher J.P. "Richard Lewis." In *Building the West: The Early Architects of British Columbia*, edited by Donald Luxton, 46–47. Vancouver: Talonbooks, 2007.

Henderson's British Columbia Gazetteer and Directory. Victoria: Henderson Publishing Company, 1898.

Henderson's Greater Victoria City Directory. Victoria: Henderson Directory Company, 1918.

Heron, Craig. *Booze: A Distilled History*. Toronto: Between the Lines, 2003.

Holloway, Godfrey. *The Empress of Victoria*. Victoria: Key Pacific Publishers, 1992.

Howard, Frederick P., and George Barnett. *British Columbia Guide and Directory for 1863*. Victoria: Office of the British Columbian and Victoria Directory, 1863.

Humphreys, Danda. *Building Victoria: Men, Myths, and Mortar*. Surrey, BC: Heritage House, 2004.

Jewell, James. "Thwarting Southern Schemes and British Bluster in the Pacific Northwest." In *Civil War Wests: Testing the Limits of the United States*, edited by Adam Arenson and Andrew Graybill, 15–32. Berkeley: University of California Press, 2015.

Johnson, Hugh J.M., ed. *The Pacific Province: A History of British Columbia*. Vancouver: Douglas & McIntyre, 1996.

Kluckner, Michael. *Victoria: The Way It Was*. North Vancouver: Whitecap Books, 1986.

Luxton, Donald, ed. *Building the West: The Early Architects of British Columbia*. Vancouver: Talonbooks, 2007.

———. "Thomas Hooper, 1857–1935." In *Building the West: The Early Architects of British Columbia*, edited by Donald Luxton, 139–45. Vancouver: Talonbooks, 2007.

Luxton, Norman. *Tilikum: Luxton's Pacific Crossing*. Toronto: Key Porter Books, 2002.

Mallandaine, Edward. *British Columbia Directory*. Victoria: Mallandaine and Williams, 1887.

Mazer, Les D. *Heritage Conservation Report for the City of Victoria*. Victoria: Ker, Priestman & Associates, 1975.

McKelvie, Bruce Alistair. "The Stone Giant." Chap. 28 in *Magic, Murder and Mystery*. Duncan, BC: Cowichan Leader, Ltd., 1966.

Mole, Rich. *Scoundrels and Saloons: Whisky Wars of the Pacific Northwest, 1840 to 1917*. Victoria: Heritage House, 2012.

Nesbitt, James K. "Bill Lush's Park Hotel." In *Victoria Old Homes and Families*. Victoria: Hebden Printing, 1956.

———. "Old Ruins Told Tales." *Islander Magazine*, September 1958.

———. "Victoria Men Whooped It Up in Swish Hotel Delmonico." *Islander Magazine*, December 31, 1967.

Oke, Nancy, and Robert Griffin. *Feeding the Family: 100 Years of Food and Drink in Victoria*. Victoria: Royal British Columbia Museum, 2011.

Ormsby, Margaret. *British Columbia: A History*. Vancouver: Macmillan, 1958.

Pashley, Nicholas. *Cheers: An Intemperate History of Beer in Canada*. Toronto: HarperCollins, 2009.

Peterson, Jan. *Kilts on the Coast: The Scots Who Built BC*. Victoria: Heritage House, 2012.

Pethick, Derek, and Susan Baumgarten. *British Columbia Recalled: A Picture History 1741–1871*. Saanichton, BC: Hancock House, 1974.

Preyde, James, and Susan Preyde. *Yukon Gold: High Hopes and Dashed Dreams*. Surrey, BC: Hancock House, 1995.

Reksten, Terry. *"More English than the English": A Very Social History of Victoria*. Victoria: Orca Book Publishers, 1986.

——. *The Empress Hotel: In the Grand Style*. Vancouver: Douglas & McIntyre, 1997.

Roy, Patricia E., ed. *A History of British Columbia: Selected Readings*. Vancouver: Copp Clark Pitman, 1989.

Segger, Martin, and Douglas Franklin. *Exploring Victoria's Architecture*. Victoria: Sono Nis Press, 1996.

Touchie, Rodger. *Vancouver Island: Portrait of a Past*. Vancouver: J.J. Douglas, 1974.

Waddington, Alfred P. *The Fraser Mines Vindicated, or, the History of Four Months*. Vancouver: Robert Reid, 1858.

Ward, W. Peter, and Robert A.J. McDonald, eds. *British Columbia: Historical Readings*. Vancouver: Douglas & McIntyre, 1981.

Winks, Robin W. *The Civil War Years: Canada and the United States*. Montreal and Kingston: McGill-Queen's University Press, 1998.

Wolfenden, Madge. "Books and Libraries in Fur-Trading and Colonial Days." *British Columbia Quarterly*, 11, no. 3 (1947): 159–86.

——. "Driard, Sosthenes Maximilian." In *Dictionary of Canadian Bibliography*, vol. 10. University of Toronto/Université Laval, 2003. http://www.biographi.ca/en/bio/driard_sosthenes_maximilian_10E.html.

ENDNOTES

INTRODUCTION

[1] Quoted in M.P. Singh, *Quote, Unquote: A Handbook of Famous Quotations* (New Delhi: Lotus Press, 2006), 124.

CHAPTER ONE: THE PIONEER SALOONS AND HOTEL BARS, 1851–59

[1] Goodreads, http://www.goodreads.com/quotes/60281-in-wine-there-is-wisdom-in-beer-there-is-freedom/.

[2] Robert A. Campbell, *Demon Rum or Easy Money: Government Control of Liquor in British Columbia from Prohibition to Privatization* (Ottawa: Carleton University Press, 1991), 10.

[3] Peter A. Baskerville, *Beyond the Island: An Illustrated History of Victoria* (Burlington, ON: Windsor Publications, 1986), 30.

[4] Michael Kluckner, *Victoria: The Way It Was* (North Vancouver: Whitecap Books, 1986), 20.

[5] Terry Reksten, *"More English than the English": A Very Social History of Victoria* (Victoria: Orca Book Publishers, 1986), 41.

[6] Jan Peterson, *Kilts on the Coast: The Scots Who Built BC* (Victoria: Heritage House, 2012), 106.

[7] *Colonial Despatches of Vancouver Island and British Columbia, 1846–1871*, 9499 305/4, Humanities and Computing Centre, University of Victoria.

[8] Alfred Waddington mentioned on page 57 of his book, *The Fraser Mines Vindicated, or, the History of Four Months* (Vancouver: Robert Reid, 1858), that he believed the wooden building south of Sutro's wholesale tobacco warehouse on the corner of Yates and Wharf Streets was Yates's Ship Inn Saloon.

[9] Peterson, *Kilts on the Coast*, 183.

[10] "Victoria's First Hotel," *British Colonist*, June 14, 1883, 3. The *British Colonist*, as it was known from 1858 to July 28, 1860, became the *Daily British Colonist* on July 31, 1860, until

December 31, 1886. From January 1, 1887, to 1946 it was the *Daily Colonist*. The name *British Colonist* is used throughout the book to represent this newspaper.

[11] *British Colonist*, August 2, 1908, 18.

[12] *British Colonist*, December 20, 1859, 1.

[13] *British Colonist*, August 12, 1859, 2.

[14] *British Colonist*, January 14, 1881, 3.

[15] Danda Humphreys, *Building Victoria: Men, Myths and Mortar* (Surrey, BC: Heritage House, 2004), 46.

[16] *British Colonist*, September 21, 1864, 3.

[17] *British Colonist*, September 13, 1860, 2.

[18] *British Colonist*, September 10, 1876, 3.

[19] Harry Gregson, *A History of Victoria, 1842–1970* (Victoria: Observer Publishing, 1970), 30.

[20] *British Colonist*, November 16, 1868, 2.

[21] *British Colonist*, February 20, 1872, 2.

[22] *British Colonist*, April 27, 1863, 3.

[23] *British Colonist*, August 6, 1863, 3.

[24] *British Colonist*, November 4, 1859, 2.

[25] "Accident," *British Colonist*, December 29, 1865, 3.

[26] *British Colonist*, September 15, 1860, 2.

[27] Cecil Clark, *The Best of Victoria, Yesterday and Today: A Nostalgic 115-Year Pictorial History of Victoria* (Victoria: The Victoria Weekly, 1973).

[28] *British Colonist*, December 5, 1884, 3.

[29] Clark, *The Best of Victoria, Yesterday and Today*.

[30] *British Colonist*, June 25, 1907, 4.

[31] T.W. Patterson, "Williams: One of Cowichan's First Tour Operators," *Cowichan Valley Citizen*, February 6, 2015.

[32] "Celebrate Their Diamond Wedding," *British Colonist*, November 26, 1911, 21.

[33] The address numbering system in Victoria changed in 1907–8 and took years to complete. Where possible throughout the book, I have shown old street numbers in parentheses along with the present numbers.

[34] *British Colonist*, February 28, 1866, 2.

35 *British Colonist*, January 15, 1859, 3.
36 *British Colonist*, June 9, 1875, 3.
37 Gregson, *A History of Victoria*, 20.
38 *British Colonist*, July 10, 1862, 3.
39 *British Colonist*, June 28, 1864, 3.
40 *British Colonist*, July 10, 1866, 2.
41 "Disastrous Fire," *British Colonist*, June 8, 1875, 3.

CHAPTER TWO: THE ROUGH EDGE OF TOWN,
1860–69

1 BrainyQuote, http://www.brainyquote.com/quotes/quotes/m/
marktwain100058.html.
2 Reksten, *"More English than the English,"* 31.
3 Baskerville, *Beyond the Island*, 44.
4 *British Colonist*, October 6, 1862, 2.
5 Rodger Touchie, *Vancouver Island: Portrait of a Past* (Vancouver:
J.J. Douglas, 1974), 44.
6 Craig Heron, *Booze: A Distilled History* (Toronto: Between the
Lines, 2003), 108.
7 Heron, *Booze*, 113.
8 *British Colonist*, January 6, 1862, 2.
9 See Kluckner, *Victoria*, 34.
10 *British Colonist*, June 19, 1866, 2.
11 "Awfully Sudden Death," *British Colonist*, December 15, 1872, 3.
12 *British Colonist*, September 5, 1884, 3.
13 Kluckner, *Victoria*, 38.
14 Valerie Green, *Upstarts and Outcasts: Victoria's Not-So-Proper
Past* (Victoria: TouchWood Editions, 2000), 160.
15 *British Colonist*, January 23, 1861, 1.
16 Green, *Upstarts and Outcasts*, 161.
17 Ronald Greene, "The Brown Jug Saloon of Victoria: Token History,"
British Columbia History Magazine, Spring 2008, 24–25.
18 "The Brown Jug," *British Colonist*, September 19, 1870, 2.
19 *British Colonist*, December 4, 1872, 3.
20 *British Colonist*, March 22, 1866, 2.
21 *British Colonist*, September 8, 1885, 3.

22 In Greene, "The Brown Jug Saloon of Victoria," 24.

23 *British Colonist*, March 5, 1861, 3.

24 For more regarding the history of organ music and Seeley's contribution, visit http://www.thecanadianencyclopedia.ca/en/article/victoria-bc-emc/.

25 Gregson, *A History of Victoria*, 16–17.

26 *British Colonist*, May 9, 1865, 3.

27 Ibid., 3.

28 *British Colonist*, February 6, 1866, 3.

29 D.W.H., "The Fight for the Standard: The Trouble That a Bit of Bunting Caused," *British Colonist*, August 23, 1903, 7.

30 *British Colonist*, November 22, 1864, 2.

31 Ibid.

32 "A Ghastly Mystery," *British Colonist*, April 24, 1881, 3.

33 *British Colonist*, November 18, 1870, 2.

34 *British Colonist*, December 20, 1870, 3.

35 "A Ghastly Mystery," *British Colonist*, April 24, 1881, 3. An excellent account of the discovery of the body beneath the floorboards of the Omineca Saloon can be found in James K. Nesbitt, "Old Ruins Told Tales," *Islander Magazine*, September 1958.

36 *British Colonist*, April 24, 1881, 3.

37 Emily Carr, *The Book of Small* (Markham, ON: Fitzhenry & Whiteside, 2004), 10–11.

38 Ibid., 11.

39 *British Colonist*, September 6, 1864, 3.

40 James K. Nesbitt, *Victoria Old Homes and Families* (Victoria: Hebden Printing, 1956), 33–36.

41 "Shocking Occurrence! Wm. Lush, Keeper of the Park Hotel, Takes Strychnine and Dies!" *British Colonist*, January 29, 1875, 1.

42 Green, *Upstarts and Outcasts*, 174.

43 *British Colonist*, September 21, 1867, 2.

44 Carr, *The Book of Small*, 88.

45 *British Colonist*, May 17, 1887, 4.

46 Bruce Alistair McKelvie, "The Stone Giant," chap. 28 in *Magic, Murder and Mystery* (Duncan, BC: Cowichan Leader, Ltd., 1966).

47 "The Stone Man," *British Colonist*, January 7, 1886, 3.

[48] Christopher J.P. Hanna, "Richard Lewis," in *Building the West: The Early Architects of British Columbia*, ed. Donald Luxton (Vancouver: Talonbooks, 2007), 46–47.

[49] "Terrible Affray—A Man Cut Open with an Axe," *British Colonist*, February 26, 1884, 3.

[50] *British Colonist*, May 7, 1892, 5.

[51] *British Colonist*, June 16, 1909, 7.

[52] Ibid.

[53] *Vancouver Daily Record*, September 16, 1913, 1.

[54] Reksten, *"More English than the English,"* 61.

[55] Frederick P. Howard and George Barnett, *British Columbia Guide and Directory for 1863* (Victoria: Office of the British Columbian and Victoria Directory, 1863), 57.

[56] "Their Golden Wedding," *British Colonist*, May 19, 1912, 5.

[57] *British Colonist*, February 23, 1872, 3.

[58] *British Colonist*, January 15, 1873, 2.

[59] Martin Segger and Douglas Franklin, *Exploring Victoria's Architecture* (Victoria: Sono Nis Press, 1996), 90.

[60] *British Colonist*, June 16, 1893, 5.

[61] "A Serious Shooting," *British Colonist*, October 12, 1895, 5.

[62] "Spring Assizes," *British Colonist*, June 20, 1896, 3.

[63] *British Colonist*, November 9, 1867, 2.

[64] *British Colonist*, September 8, 1875, 1.

[65] "New Quarters," *British Colonist*, January 10, 1879, 3.

[66] "Mike Powers Knew His Slayer," *British Colonist*, October 7, 1899, 2; Cecil Clark, "Mike Powers Wouldn't Talk," *Islander Magazine*, January 23, 1972, 7–8.

[67] "Mike Powers Knew His Slayer," 2; "Who Slew Mike Powers?" *British Colonist*, October 8, 1899, 1.

[68] I explain the events that led to the decision and the legislation in detail in Chapter Five.

[69] *Vancouver Daily Building Record*, July 10, 1913, 1.

CHAPTER THREE: STRICTLY FIRST-CLASS

[1] King James Version.

[2] Green, *Upstarts and Outcasts*, 127.

[3] Green, *Upstarts and Outcasts*, 163.

[4] *British Colonist*, December 4, 1862, 3.

[5] *British Colonist*, December 15, 1862, 1; Madge Wolfenden, "Books and Libraries in Fur-Trading and Colonial Days," *British Columbia Quarterly*, 11, no. 3 (1947): 165.

[6] James Jewell, "Thwarting Southern Schemes and British Bluster in the Pacific Northwest," in *Civil War Wests: Testing the Limits of the United States*, ed. Adam Arenson and Andrew Graybill (Berkeley: University of California Press, 2015), 15–32.

[7] Robin W. Winks, *The Civil War Years: Canada and the United States* (Montreal and Kingston: McGill-Queen's University Press, 1998), 164.

[8] John Masters and Horizon Writers' Group, "Victoria Celebrates 150 Years," *Toronto Sun*, July 22, 2012, http://www.torontosun.com/2012/07/20/victoria-celebrates150-years/.

[9] *British Colonist*, May 21, 1867, 3.

[10] *British Colonist*, January 30, 1868, 4.

[11] *British Colonist*, June 26, 1879, 3.

[12] *British Colonist*, April 10, 1894, 5.

[13] *British Colonist*, April 26, 1862, 3.

[14] *British Colonist*, July 10, 1865, 2.

[15] Segger and Franklin, *Exploring Victoria's Architecture*, 35.

[16] *British Colonist*, January 10, 1884, 2.

[17] Green, *Upstarts and Outcasts*, 163.

[18] Ibid., 164.

[19] Ibid., 166.

[20] Madge Wolfenden, "Driard, Sosthenes Maximilian," in *Dictionary of Canadian Biography*, vol. 10, University of Toronto/Université Laval, 2003, http://www.biographi.ca/en/bio/driard_sosthenes_maximilian_10E.html.

[21] "The Death of Driard," *British Colonist*, February 16, 1873, 3.

[22] "Disastrous Fire," *British Colonist*, June 8, 1875, 3.

[23] "Fire This Morning," *British Colonist*, October 1, 1882, 3.

[24] Green, *Upstarts and Outcasts*, 167.

[25] Kluckner, *Victoria*, 35.

[26] Carr, *The Book of Small*, 163.

27 "Hotel Accommodation," *British Colonist*, March 24, 1883, 2.

28 "The Driard Bar," *British Colonist*, May 13, 1892, 5.

29 Kluckner, *Victoria*, 35.

30 Terry Reksten, *The Empress Hotel: In the Grand Style* (Vancouver: Douglas & McIntyre, 1997), 42.

31 "Flames Sweep City's Business Centre," *British Colonist*, 1910, 1–2.

32 *British Colonist*, December 1, 1876, 3.

33 *British Colonist*, November 21, 1893, 5.

34 *British Colonist*, August 17, 1890, 5.

35 *British Colonist*, January 16, 1898, 5.

36 *British Colonist*, September 28, 1898, 5.

37 "The Clarence, Victoria's New Hotel," *British Colonist*, September 4, 1886, 3.

38 *British Colonist*, December 24, 1887, 2.

39 "A Pistol Bullet Terminates the Life of a Young Victorian," *British Colonist*, February 21, 1890, 1.

40 *British Colonist*, April 5, 1888, 4.

41 *British Colonist*, February 1, 1898, 5.

42 "Suffocated by Gas," *British Colonist*, February 15, 1898, 7.

43 Barry Elmer and Dorothy Mindenhall, "Edward McCoskrie, 1822–1893," in *Building the West: The Early Architects of British Columbia*, ed. Donald Luxton (Vancouver: Talonbooks, 2007), 163.

44 Gregson, *A History of Victoria*, 132.

45 Alfred Emberson, *Victoria Illustrated* (Victoria: Ellis & Co., 1891), 89.

46 *British Colonist*, January 10, 1892, 5.

47 "Against Prohibition," *British Colonist*, September 28, 5.

48 *British Colonist*, July 14, 1900, 5.

49 *British Colonist*, August 3, 1900, 6.

50 *British Colonist*, December 20, 1907, 7.

51 Green, *Upstarts and Outcasts*, 172.

52 "A Splendid Hotel," *British Colonist*, March 30, 1892, 5.

53 Donald Luxton, "Thomas Hooper, 1857–1935," in *Building the West: The Early Architects of British Columbia*, ed. Donald Luxton (Vancouver: Talonbooks, 2007), 140.

54 *British Colonist*, April 29, 1892, 5.

[55] An excellent account of the voyage can be found in Norman Luxton, *Tilikum: Luxton's Pacific Crossing* (Toronto: Key Porter Books, 2002).

[56] This is the historical term that was used in 1900.

[57] For more on Captain Voss see John M. MacFarlane, "Captain John Claus Voss FRGS," *Nauticapedia*, 2002, http://nauticapedia.ca/ Articles/Tilikum_Voss.php.

[58] *British Colonist*, October 8, 1898, 5.

[59] *British Colonist*, September 2, 1915, 6.

[60] *British Colonist*, July 1, 1905, 5.

[61] *British Colonist*, December 17, 1905, 11.

[62] *British Colonist*, December 25, 1905, 5.

[63] *British Colonist*, December 16, 1906, 14; "King Edward Hotel," *Canada's Historic Places* (n.d.), http://www.historicplaces.ca/en/ rep-reg/place-lieu.aspx?id=15619.

[64] *British Colonist*, February 10, 1910, 2.

[65] *British Colonist*, April 3, 1915, 7.

[66] Reksten, *The Empress Hotel*, 17. Reksten's book is the definitive source about the Empress Hotel from the planning stage to 1990.

[67] "To Build the Tourist Hotel," *British Colonist*, December 1, 1903, 1.

[68] Reksten, *The Empress Hotel*, 19.

[69] Ibid., 27.

[70] Ibid., 37.

[71] Les D. Mazer, *Heritage Conservation Report for the City of Victoria* (Victoria: Ker, Priestman & Associates, 1975), 35.

[72] Reksten, *The Empress Hotel*, 42.

[73] Godfrey Holloway, *The Empress of Victoria* (Victoria: Key Pacific Publishers, 1992), 11.

[74] Segger and Franklin, *Exploring Victoria's Architecture*, 61.

[75] Reksten, *The Empress Hotel*, 55.

[76] Campbell, *Demon Rum or Easy Money*, 18.

CHAPTER FOUR: THE GOLDEN AGE, 1870–99

[1] Faust Distributing Company, Toasts and Quotes, http://www. faustdistributing.com/just-for-fun/toasts-quotes.

[2] Touchie, *Vancouver Island*, 44.

3 The Victoria Police Department charge book for April to November 1875 shows the number of incidents of public drunkenness; it can be assessed at http://contentdm.library.uvic.ca/cdm/compoundob-ject/collection/collection7/id/930/rec/1.

4 Green, *Upstarts and Outcasts*, 127.

5 "Potted Chicken, Who Stole Mrs. Murphy's Rooster?" *British Colonist*, September 11, 1889, 4.

6 James K. Nesbitt, "Victoria Men Whooped It Up in Swish Hotel Delmonico," *Islander Magazine*, December 31, 1967, 2, 13.

7 Peter Grant, *Victoria: A History in Photographs* (Vancouver: Altitude Publishing, 1995), 46.

8 Numerous books have been written about the Klondike Gold Rush. One of my favourites is by Pierre Berton, *Klondike: The Last Great Gold Rush, 1896–1899* (Toronto: McClelland & Stewart, 1972).

9 *British Colonist*, November 19, 1864, 3.

10 *British Colonist*, August 14, 1867, 3.

11 The fire occurred sometime between January and March 1889 and completely destroyed the wood structure.

12 *Annual Reports of the Corporation of the City of Victoria for the Year Ending 31st December 1891*, 7, https://books.google.ca/books?id=4f84AQAAMAAJ.

13 "Licensing Board," *British Colonist*, March 16, 1889, 1.

14 *British Colonist*, July 17, 1891, 5.

15 *British Colonist*, July 19, 1904, 5.

16 *British Colonist*, March 16, 1881, 3.

17 "History of Whaling," *Wikipedia*, last modified January 21, 2016, https://en.wikipedia.org/wiki/History_of_whaling.

18 "By the Sad Sea Waves—The Spirit of Another Pioneer Takes Flight," *British Colonist*, March 16, 1881, 3.

19 *British Colonist*, March 17, 1881, 3.

20 *British Colonist*, August 8, 1894, 5.

21 *British Colonist*, December 9, 1900, 2.

22 "Uses Bottle with Vicious Intent—Italians Badly Cut by Country-Man in Bar Room Fracas, Assailant Still at Large in the City," *British Colonist*, July 11, 1911, 8.

23 *British Colonist*, January 24, 1971, 2.

24 *British Colonist*, April 9, 1872, 1.

25 *British Colonist*, September 2, 1877, 3.

26 *British Colonist*, March 9, 1925, 1.

27 *British Colonist*, April 18, 1908, 7.

28 "Badly Beaten in Drunken Street Brawl," *British Colonist*, August 27, 1907, 2.

29 "Makes Two Attempts to Strangle Himself," *British Colonist*, September 6, 1908, 7.

30 *British Colonist*, December 2, 1909, 3.

31 *British Colonist*, August 5, 1879, 3.

32 *British Colonist*, December 17, 1879, 2.

33 *British Colonist*, March 20, 1889, 4.

34 *British Colonist*, October 21, 1897, 8.

35 *British Colonist*, August 5, 1902, 7; December 2, 1902, 6.

36 *Vancouver Daily Building Record*, January 3, 1914, 3.

37 *British Colonist*, July 5, 1870, 2.

38 Segger and Franklin, *Exploring Victoria's Architecture*, 94.

39 Alexander Caulfield Anderson, *British Columbia Directory, 1882–1883* (Victoria: R.T. Williams, 1883), 14.

40 *British Colonist*, April 17, 1885, 1.

41 "The Fire Fiend," *British Colonist*, April 17, 1885, 3.

42 *British Colonist*, November 18, 1897, 5.

43 *British Colonist*, April 30, 1898, 5.

44 "The Ever-Ready Knife," *British Colonist*, April 20, 1897, 8.

45 *British Colonist*, April 22, 1897, 5.

46 "Hotel Keepers Are Heavily Penalized," *British Colonist*, November 30, 1916, 5.

47 *British Colonist*, October 24, 1899, 5.

48 *British Colonist*, April 19, 1901, 3.

49 Rich Mole, *Scoundrels and Saloons: Whisky Wars of the Pacific Northwest, 1840 to 1917* (Victoria: Heritage House, 2012), 89–90.

50 *British Colonist*, April 4, 1891, 4.

51 *British Colonist*, November 9, 1900, 6.

52 *British Colonist*, July 4, 1907, 3.

53 *British Colonist*, October 21, 1911, 7.

54 *British Colonist*, March 24, 1892, 2.

55 *British Colonist*, December 17, 1891, 5.
56 *British Colonist*, April 20, 1894, 5.
57 Information provided by Paul Hutchinson, the great-nephew of Alexander and Mary Simpson; Jean Hepburn furnished information for the 1881 census that confirmed Hutchinson's insights.
58 "Stokes-Simpson," *British Colonist*, February 4, 1903, 2.
59 Information provided by Alan Newberry, the grandson of Alexander Hesson.
60 Hotels offered guests the European plan, which meant sharing a common bathroom down the hall for a reduced rate, or the American plan, which included an en-suite bathroom.
61 Rosemary James Cross, "Lord Wilfrid Hargreaves," in *Building the West: The Early Architects of British Columbia*, ed. Donald Luxton (Vancouver: Talonbooks, 2007), 365.
62 *British Colonist*, December 23, 1913, 5.

CHAPTER FIVE: RESTRICTION TO PROHIBITION, 1900–17

1 BrainyQuote, http://www.brainyquote.com/quotes/quotes/s/stephenlea153181.html.
2 Campbell, *Demon Rum or Easy Money*, 18.
3 Harold Tuttle Allen, *Forty Years' Journey: The Temperance Movement in British Columbia to 1900* (Victoria: Self-published, 1982), 7.
4 See Douglas L. Hamilton, "British Columbia's First Liquor Prohibition: Natives and Alcohol, 1854–1962," chap. 2 in *Sobering Dilemma: A History of Prohibition in British Columbia* (Vancouver: Ronsdale Press, 2004), 37–61.
5 Campbell, *Demon Rum or Easy Money*, 12.
6 Robert A. Campbell, *Sit Down and Drink Your Beer: Regulating Vancouver's Beer Parlours, 1925–1954* (Toronto: University of Toronto Press, 2001), 17.
7 Hamilton, *Sobering Dilemma*, 76.
8 Baskerville, *Beyond the Island*, 170.
9 Campbell, *Sit Down and Drink Your Beer*, 17.
10 *The Vancouver Daily Building Record*, December 6, 1913, 2.

[11] Campbell, *Demon Rum or Easy Money*, 22.

[12] Hamilton, *Sobering Dilemma*, 91.

[13] *British Colonist*, July 8, 1888, 1.

[14] *British Colonist*, February 4, 1904, 1.

[15] *Victoria Daily Times*, April 17, 1904, 5.

[16] *British Colonist*, July 24, 1907, 1.

[17] *British Colonist*, October 27, 1912, 34.

[18] *British Colonist*, July 12, 1916, 2.

[19] *British Colonist*, October 23, 1920, 1.

[20] Segger and Franklin, *Exploring Victoria's Architecture*, 42.

[21] Elizabeth Gordon, "Colourful Simeon Duck," *Islander Magazine*, January 24, 2010, http://victoriahistory.ca/blog/2010/06/colourful-simeon-duck/.

[22] Gordon, "Colourful Simeon Duck."

[23] Stephen Ruttan, "Stella: When Only the Best Will Do," Greater Victoria Public Library, July 2008, https://gvpl.ca/using-the-library/our-collection/local-history/tales-from-the-vault/stella-when-only-the-best-will-do.

[24] Tom Hawthorn, "Victoria's Colourful History of Sex for Sale," *Globe and Mail*, October 26, 2010, http://www.theglobeandmail.com/news/british-columbia/victorias-colourful-history-of-sex-for-sale/article4330710/.

[25] "Amateur Boxing Will Be Boomed," *British Colonist*, November 13, 1908, 9.

[26] *British Colonist*, February 5, 1919, 5.

[27] *British Colonist*, June 19, 1918, 5.

[28] *British Colonist*, July 17, 1891, 2.

[29] "The Balmoral," *British Colonist*, May 20, 1892, 5.

[30] *Henderson's British Columbia Gazetteer and Directory* (Victoria: Henderson Publishing Company, 1898), 660.

[31] *British Colonist*, September 14, 1898, 2.

[32] *British Colonist*, October 17, 1894, 5.

[33] *British Colonist*, March 3, 1893, 5.

[34] *British Colonist*, October 24, 1912, 18.

[35] Receipt books of Silver Spring Brewery Limited, April 30 to May 28, 1911, author's personal collection.

[36] Gregson, *A History of Victoria*, 216.

[37] *British Colonist*, June 6, 1913, 1–2.

[38] Greg Evans wrote his master's thesis on the history of breweries in Victoria; see his blog at https://bcbrews.wordpress.com/tag/greg-evans/.

[39] For more insight into the Lion Brewery Tap Saloon under Fairbrother's proprietorship, see http://privat.bahnhof.se/wb910410/4556530b-d0d6-45ec-9e74-b03b86eb881f-9.html.

[40] "Quaint Character Removed by Death," *British Colonist*, January 20, 1917, 7.

[41] *British Colonist*, March 11, 1909, 2.

[42] *British Colonist*, March 11, 1911, 7.

[43] *British Colonist*, June 10, 1911, 3.

[44] *British Colonist*, July 15, 1911, 7.

[45] *British Colonist*, July 22, 1911, 3.

[46] *British Colonist*, December 8, 1914, 6.

[47] "Old Landmark Turned to New Use," *British Colonist*, February 24, 1916, 6.

[48] "Driard and Theatre Sold," *British Colonist*, November 10, 1910, 1.

[49] *British Colonist*, April 22, 1911, 10.

[50] "Last Word in Palatial Restaurants—The New Songhees Grill," *British Colonist*, August 24, 1911, 15.

[51] Ibid.

[52] "Social and Personal," *British Colonist*, August 29, 1911, 6.

[53] Information provided by Patty Durdle, granddaughter of K.A. Ray.

[54] "Cider Proves Strong Bone of Contention," *British Colonist*, November 6, 1917, 7.

[55] "Lim Bang: A Victoria-Born Chinese in Local Business and Chinese Politics," *Victoria's Chinatown*, http://chinatown.library.uvic.ca/lim_bang.

[56] "Prince George Hotel," *British Colonist*, January 24, 1912, 6.

[57] "Hotel Effects Sold," *British Colonist*, July 26, 1912, 6.

[58] "Shoots Himself as Police Enter Room," *British Colonist*, June 28, 1913, 7.

[59] *British Colonist*, July 4, 1913, 7.

[60] *British Colonist*, December 30, 1914, 5.

[61] *Henderson's Greater Victoria City Directory* (Victoria: Henderson Directory Company, 1918).

[62] Ronald Greene, "Token History: The Kaiserhof Hotel," *British Columbia Historical News*, July 2003, 38–39.

[63] Donald Luxton, "Thomas Hooper."

[64] Segger and Franklin, *Exploring Victoria's Architecture*, 67.

[65] *British Colonist*, January 19, 1913, 6.

[66] *British Colonist*, January 19, 1913, 5.

[67] *British Colonist*, April 2–10, 1913, ran clever ads promoting the Kaiserhof Hotel.

[68] Greene, "Token History," 38.

[69] *British Colonist*, October 17, 1914, 8.

[70] *British Colonist*, September 16, 1915, 6.

[71] Greene, "Token History."

[72] Hamilton, *Sobering Dilemma*, 197.

CONCLUSION: THE BOTTOM OF THE GLASS

[1] W.C. Fields in the film *My Little Chickadee*, 1940, https://en.wikiquote.org/wiki/W._C._Fields.

[2] Green, *Upstarts and Outcasts*, 115.

[3] Campbell, *Demon Rum*, 24.

[4] Hamilton, *Sobering Dilemma*, 194.

ACKNOWLEDGEMENTS

I began researching this book in 1999, and so I'd like to thank the staff of the British Columbia Archives, the Esquimalt Archives, the City of Victoria Archives, and the Greater Victoria Public Library for their excellent assistance during all that time.

I am indebted to the University of Victoria Digital Collection for providing online access to the *British Colonist* newspapers from 1858 to 1910, and the Vancouver Public Library for providing the British Columbia Directories from 1860 to 1955, also online. I'm grateful for the newspaper columns by James K. Nesbitt and Cecil Clark, which have provided hours of pleasant reading and interesting facts. History books and articles written by John Adams, Valerie Green, Terry Reksten, Michael Kluckner, Ronald Greene, Carey Pallister, Danda Humphreys, Rodger Touchie, and Aaron Chapman have influenced me and provided important material for this book.

I also wish to extend a very warm thank you to the following persons who donated their time, either by researching or by contributing material for this book: Selene Higgins, Lotus Johnson, Patti Doherty, Karen Howard, Jason Vanderhill, Eric Gandy, and Paul Hutcheson. I must also express my gratitude to Gordon Friesen for the fine artwork he's provided.

I extend a special thank you to Taryn Boyd and Touchwood Editions for picking up my manuscript and encouraging me during the whole process, and to Lana Okerlund for her patience and professional work during the editing process.

Finally, I thank the gang at the Tally-Ho pub in Victoria, who provided an appreciative audience during my elaborate and, at times, longwinded stories about the watering holes of the past. I look forward to hoisting a beer with you all.

INDEX

GLEN A. MOFFORD is a historian and writer with a passion for sharing the social history of British Columbia. He graduated from Vancouver's Simon Fraser University, and has been writing about BC's historic hotels and their drinking establishments for more than ten years. *Aqua Vitae* is his first book. Follow him on Twitter at @BCPubHistory, and visit his blog at raincoasthistory.blogspot.ca.